THE BOAT BUFF'S BOOK OF EMBROIDERY

Books by Carter Houck and Myron Miller

THE BOAT BUFF'S BOOK OF EMBROIDERY

THE BIG BAG BOOK

AMERICAN QUILTS AND HOW TO MAKE THEM

THE BOAT BUFF'S BOOK OF EMBROIDERY

NEEDLEPOINT - CREWEL - APPLIQUÉ

Carter Houck & Myron Miller

Charles Scribner's Sons · New York

To *Cottontail,* number 64, a Herreshoff S-boat,
and to all the races that she sailed,
no matter whether she won or lost

We want to thank all the people who gave us a hand and cheered us on: the D.M.C. Corporation, Effie Miller, Linda Houck, Sharon Valiant, Herb and Marge Meyer, Martha Ann Crowe, and boat companies too numerous to mention.

Line art and graphs by Francine Del Re

Library of Congress Cataloging in Publication Data
Houck, Carter.
The boat buff's book of embroidery.
1. Needlework—Patterns. 2. Embroidery—Patterns.
3. Design, Decorative—Themes, Motives. 4. Boats and boating.
I. Miller, Myron, 1918- joint author. II. Title.
TT753.H68 746.4'4 78-22049 ISBN 0-684-16051-X

1 3 5 7 9 11 13 15 17 19 M D/C 20 18 16 14 12 10 8 6 4 2

Printed in the United States of America

Designed by Bobye List

Contents

SUPPLIERS

To find a store near you where the products used in this book are available, write:

For D.M,C. threads and yarns:
The D.M.C. Corporation
107 Trumbull St.
Elizabeth, N.J. 07206

For Pellon ® Phun Phelt ™ (banners, Plate 3)
Pellon Corporation
1120 Avenue of the Americas
New York, N.Y. 10036

For information on buying perforated paper by mail order (note cards, Plate 8):
Sewmakers, Inc.
1619 Grand Ave.
Baldwin, N.Y. 11510

Boats, an American Love Affair

Ah, boats, the stuff our dreams are made of. They may even be a part of the reality of our lives. At the least they are dropped into our conversation every day. Art, literature, history, and the daily news are filled with boats and ships, literally and metaphorically. We are no longer apt to speak in grandiose terms of "the ship of state," but we're very likely to say, "We're all in the same boat."

As children, most of us sailed vicariously through John Masefield's poems or Robert Louis Stevenson's books or as Captain Ahab in the movies. In our great American dream we have not only two cars in the garage but a boat on a trailer in the driveway. Most of us, when we're dreaming our biggest and best dreams, see ourselves owning an ocean-going yacht, complete with crew serving drinks on the afterdeck. There are other sailors who want no part of professional crews but dream of their very own 12-Meter, handled by strong young volunteers who will never set a spinnaker wrong and who willingly accept all the abuse that the owner-skipper can hand out.

There may even be quite a number of people who actually hate boats, or would if they got on them, but who dream of them all the same. One summer when I was crewing on a center-board racing boat every weekend and spending the rest of the week nursing my skinned shins and bruised knees, I had a conversation with such a person. She was a lady who resented anything akin to physical discomfort and who sat on the beach in her neat little folding chair under her lovely large folding umbrella and looked dreamily out to sea. She said, "I envy you for your sailing. I've always thought it would be such a peaceful way to travel, just gliding along with the breeze." I looked at the callouses on my hands and decided to leave her further education to someone braver than I.

For all the dreamers of ships and exploration and ocean voyages there was suddenly the Bicentennial Operation Sail. It drew enormous crowds, rave reviews, and articles in every major publication. We all longed for an age we'd never known, stripped of course of its less attractive aspects, such as three-month bouts of seasickness and few sanitary facilities. Suddenly everyone knew a square-rigger from a topsail schooner and a caravel from a ketch.

Since World War II, lakes have appeared in dry deserts all over the country, spawning a whole new group of boat enthusiasts. Some of the most arid states now have the highest per capita number of boats. Runabouts and Sailfish abound where formerly a frog would not have ventured.

America has definitely gone to sea or at least taken to the lakes, rivers, and ponds. The backs of shirts and the seats of jeans sport lovingly embroidered nautical symbols. Sofa pillows, shower curtains, and little needlepoint pictures often display the family's interest in racing, cruising, or just admiring boats from the sidelines.

It would be impossible to depict every style and type and make of craft now in use in America, let alone the dream boats of long ago. So we will have to work with representative designs of runabouts or schooners or board boats. We certainly must include ocean liners and tugboats and the great square-riggers of yesteryear. There may be a lighthouse in your life, or memories of a buoy not well rounded in a race. All these things must take their place in a book of nautical embroidery. Code flags are a necessity for signing your work or marking someone's favorite possession.

With a little change of line here or there, you should be able to alter the designs in this book to suit your own needs. Or you might start from scratch, as shown on page 24, to work out a diagram from a photograph of your favorite boat. It's not hard to think of ways to personalize a picture—a sail number or the right colored hull—so that it brings to mind a specific cruise, a terrifying race, or the dream that will be fulfilled next year.

Materials, Techniques, and Tips

Simplicity is the aim of this book—embroidery that anyone can do with a little practice. The designs and the stitches are both planned for boat buffs, not for people who win needlework prizes. It should be fun, not drudgery, to whip up a stitchery boat for a shirt or a needlepoint ship for a pillow. There is room for your own needs and imagination in the use of the designs. You should not feel restricted to a kit approach.

The graphed designs are suitable for needlepoint, cross-stitch, and rugs. The line drawings are suitable for stitchery of many kinds, using only the basic stitches described. They can be enlarged, either photostatically or on the handy graphs, page 90, and used for appliqué. Some of the detail may be left out for appliqué, or it may be worked in with those same simple stitches.

THREAD AND YARN

All the designs photographed are worked in D.M.C. yarns and threads. The cotton six-strand is Mouliné Spécial. The other cotton thread is D.M.C. Pearl, which comes in several weights, allowing you to make some interesting variations in stitchery. The Persian yarn is Floralia, which is three-ply and can be divided into any number of strands for crewel or on canvas of varying sizes. Laine Colbert D.M.C. is an ideal weight for 10-mesh canvas work. The heaviest, Laine à broder, is excellent wool rug yarn.

Examples of these yarns in use are:

Power boat on cover—Mouliné Spécial on fine linen

Sailfish on cover—two strands of Floralia on 18-mesh canvas

Drake's Galleon, Plate 6—Floralia on coarse linen

Queen Elizabeth II, Plate 7—Laine Colbert D.M.C., single strand on 10-mesh canvas

Tugboat rug, Plate 4—Laine à broder doubled on 5-mesh canvas

Racing schooner, page 52—three weights Pearl Cotton, couched single strand

1.
2.
3.
4a.
4b.
5a.
5b.
5c.

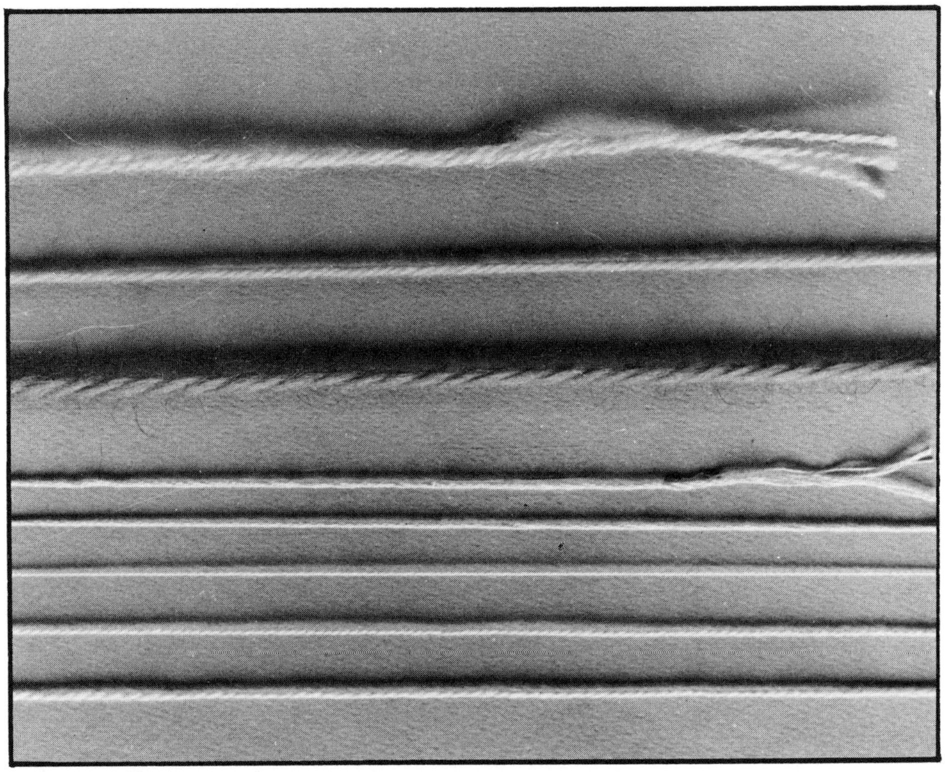

1. Floralia
2. Laine Colbert
3. Laine à broder

4a & b. Mouliné Spécial 6-strand

5a, b, c. Pearl Cotton in 3 weights

FABRICS AND CANVAS

Canvas has a more limited range than fabric, so let's deal with it first. It is a firmly woven, openly spaced base for needlepoint. The number of spaces per inch determines the mesh size. Five-mesh means five stitches to the inch, 18-mesh means eighteen stitches to the inch—between the two there is quite a difference in the yarn used, the amount of work involved, and the detail achieved in the final effect. We have attempted to keep our designs almost as simple as those in a child's coloring book so that they can be worked quickly and effectively on the larger canvas with heavier thread. If you want to add more shading and detail, you will find that it works better on finer canvas.

The largest mesh canvas is useful for rugs but is also known as quickpoint canvas; it is 3½-mesh, 5-mesh, and 7-mesh. The tugboat rug is worked on 5-mesh, using the yarn doubled to produce a good sturdy rug. Extra thickness and a firm backing were achieved by working in the basketweave form of the tent stitch.

Most needlepoint is worked on 10-mesh, 12-mesh, or 14-mesh. The Laine Colbert D.M.C., used single, is a perfect weight for 10-mesh and can be used on 12-mesh. Experiment with two to three strands of Floralia for any of these canvases, depending on which version of the tent stitch you are using. Petit-point canvas starts at 18-mesh, which may be worked with one or two strands of Floralia. The finer canvases can be worked with one strand of Floralia or with several strands of Mouliné Spécial—test first for the effect you want.

Canvas falls into three categories, depending on the construction—mono, two-thread or dual, and leno. The illustrations should help you to recognize the differences.

Mono canvas is sometimes called single-mesh because it is woven with only one thread each way. It is easy to work on and available in many sizes. The basic tent stitch can only be worked on it by the continental or basketweave methods. The less desirable half-cross will slip between the thread crossings.

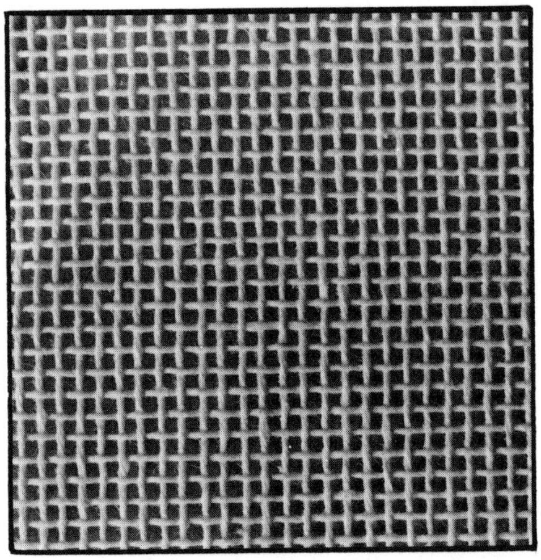

Two-thread or dual—sometimes called penelope—has, as indicated, two threads close together each way. True penelope is slightly heavier than some other available two-thread, so the threads can be divided safely and worked over singly. This creates a petit-point effect for fine detail within the larger gauge—an area of 20-to-the-inch within a 10-mesh penelope, for instance.

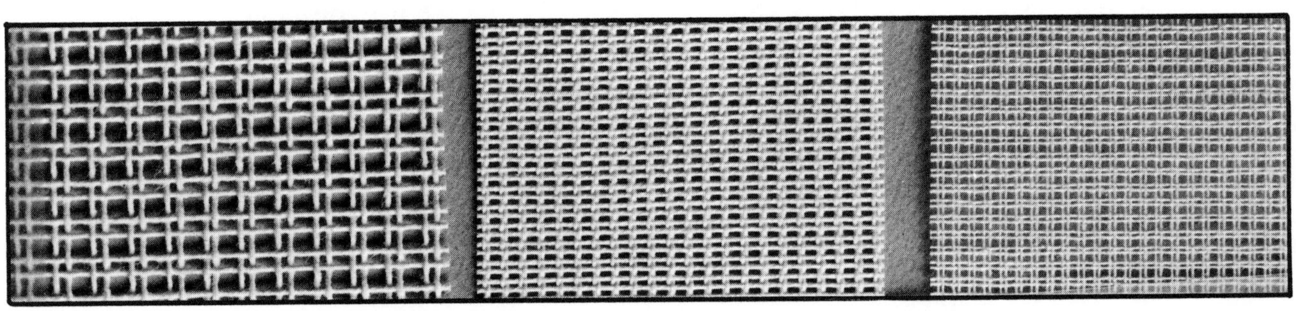

Leno canvas is usually found in the very large and very small gauges. The best 5-mesh rug canvases and the tiniest petit point, 24-mesh and smaller, are found in leno weaves. Leno is a two-thread canvas that looks at first glance like mono, because the warp threads are twisted together once between every weft thread, making a base that is firmer than any other canvas.

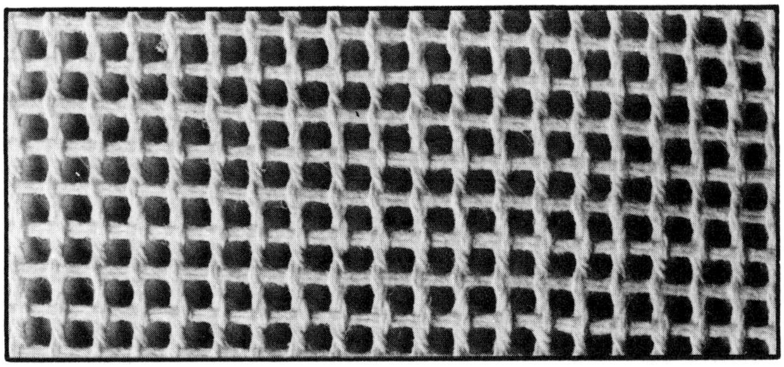

There is a type of penelope called French canvas, which is white with a blue thread every fifth line, making counted-thread cross-stitch possible on fabrics too fine or too unevenly woven to allow the counting of threads. The canvas is marked, basted on the fabric, and then pulled away—one thread at a time—after the cross-stitch is worked. See page 21.

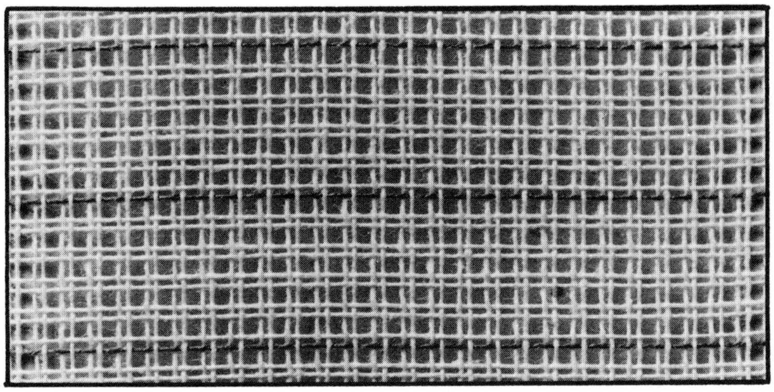

An interesting entry to the world of charted designs and counted thread is perforated paper. It was popular with Victorians and for many years before in parts of Europe, then disappeared after World War II. It has reappeared and is now available in the same 15-mesh

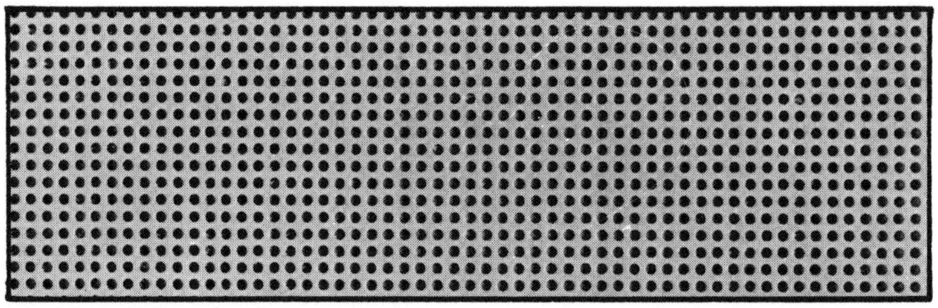

size that you may see in museums. In spite of the gauge being delicate, it is extremely easy to work on because of its evenness and the high visibility of the holes. It serves as a fine learning tool and an amusing way to work designs for greeting cards, small pictures, and bookmarks. Traditionally the background is left unworked, a great saving in time.

Fabrics for stitchery, appliqué, and counted-thread work are harder to identify than canvas. There are a few tests you can run to make sure that the fabric is suitable to the job.

For stitchery it is necessary to have a relatively firm weave and to choose a thread compatible with the texture. Shirt fabrics and T-shirt knits should be worked in one of the cotton threads, preferably Mouliné Spécial in most cases. Heavy linen, burlap, and other highly textured fabrics are effectively worked in wool yarns. Floralia has the same advantage for stitchery that Mouliné Spécial has—it can be used in varying numbers of strands.

Appliqué requires a background that is firm but not too heavy. It is more important to choose the appliqué fabric with care. There are two qualities to look for—flexibility and a close weave. The edges must turn easily and the corners must not ravel. Pure cotton is often easier to work with than a cotton blend—either can be rinsed in a fabric softener before cutting so that it will be more workable.

Fabric for counted-thread work must be an even weave, such as Hardanger. If you want to do cross-stitch on any other fabric, apply French canvas, page 7.

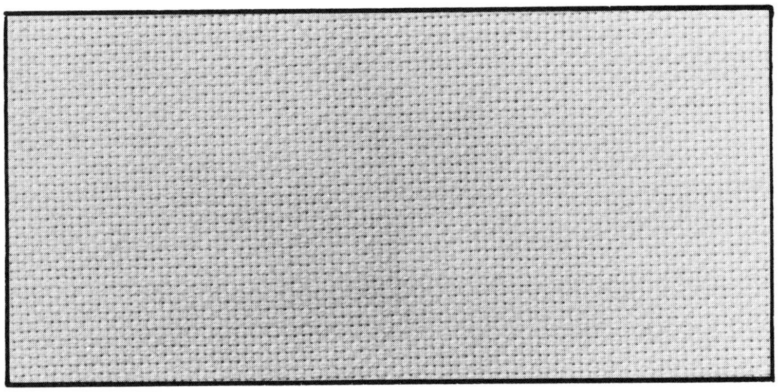

If you want to make banners and quick-and-easy pictures of boats for a child's room, you will find felt colorful and easy to work with. The pieces can be machine appliquéd or even glued. Some boat shapes lend themselves more readily to this very bold treatment than others. The distinctive shape of a Hudson River sloop translates into felt appliqué with no detail, Plate 3.

In T-shirt embroidery, the trick is to stretch the fabric as taut and smooth as it will be on the body. Start with a pure cotton T-shirt and stretch the area to be embroidered over a thin woven cotton batiste or similar fabric in a hoop or frame. Baste the two fabrics together so that they will remain just the way you want them.

Remember to choose all fabrics, canvas, and yarn or thread for compatibility. When in doubt of anything, test!

EQUIPMENT

There is so little equipment necessary for embroidery that it hardly seems worth mentioning. You should shop for needles to learn what the different kinds look like. Most people prefer a "short" or a "sharp" for appliqué. Stitchery should be done with "embroidery" or "crewel" needles. The first two needles mentioned have a round eye and are small and sharp. The second two are about the same size as the first except that the long eye makes them slightly thicker at the head. Needle sizes (the actual thickness) run counter to the size numbers—the smaller the size number, the larger the needle. The best rule is to choose the smallest-size needle that will accommodate your choice of yarn or thread. Needles that are too thick can damage the fabric.

Tapestry needles are used for any canvas work. They are long-eyed and blunt. For rug canvas you can even use the big finishing needles that are used in knitting.

It is nice to have a roomy, attractive workbag to keep your current project in. It's more fun to design your own—with signal flag monogram, perhaps—than to buy one. In it you should keep a pair of good sharp embroidery scissors that are yours and yours alone. They should be in a small case or side pocket to prevent the point from damaging your work.

A hoop or frame is absolutely necessary for stitchery. There are many on the market, and you will have to choose for yourself. For most small projects a round or oval hand-held frame is perfect and will fit in your workbag. You will find a standing frame useful for large pieces. There are also standing rug frames that make large pieces of rug canvas manageable.

If you're doing very fine embroidery, especially counted-thread, get a magnifying glass that hangs around your neck or sits on the table. If the lights in your house are all planned for decorator effect rather than good vision, buy a small direct light such as a Tensor or an art light.

The only other equipment that you will need consists of the usual things that you use for any sewing: a thimble, some measuring tools, and a few pins.

ENLARGING AND MARKING

Enlarging or reducing the graphed designs does not present a problem. They are shown in the book 10-to-the-inch (except pages 53 and

79). If you work them on 5-mesh canvas, they will automatically be doubled in size. If you work them on 18-mesh, they will automatically be reduced to almost one-half—five-ninths, to be exact. French cross-stitch canvas comes in mesh sizes like needlepoint canvas, which makes it possible to scale the designs in the same way.

Scaling the sketched designs can be done by hand, using the graphs given on page 90. Trace the design from the book on tissue or transparent tracing paper and clip it in place over the ¼-inch graph. (For ease in handling, make up several copies of each graph page on a copying machine.) Lay another piece of tracing paper on the ½-inch graph and draw the lines into the larger squares exactly as they appear in the smaller ones. The design will then be doubled in size. It can be increased to three times its original size on the ¾-inch graph. When you're through, you will only have to tidy the lines a little, using a straight ruler and a curved ruler. You can have designs photostatically enlarged—for a price.

Marking the design on fabric or canvas requires no special artistic ability but does demand care. The needlepoint designs do not have to be marked in their entirety. Many people find it easy enough to copy by counting the squares as they go, working the designs in first and then filling the background. Keep the book close by and count the squares for each color. You may need to mark a few ends and corners as a guide and then count off the rest.

If you want to paint the entire canvas, be sure to use waterproof paint. There are types made especially for this purpose, usually sold in needlework shops, and others also guaranteed washable that are sold in art stores. If in doubt, test on a scrap of canvas and then soak in warm water.

The first step in transferring the designs for stitchery is to trace them onto tissue or transparent tracing paper. You may then use *washable* dressmaker's carbon and the point of a knitting needle to transfer the design to the fabric. There are now iron-on pencils with which you can draw the design on the back of the tissue after having traced it onto the tissue from the book. Use it according to the directions with the pencil or as you would any other iron-on transfer.

Light fabrics can be traced over the tissue on a light box. This need be nothing more than a piece of glass suspended between two thick books, with a small night light on an extension cord underneath. Put the tissue down first and the fabric on top of it, then trace with a dressmaker's pencil or sharpened chalk pencil.

With any of the methods described, testing on scrap is advisable before proceeding on a good piece of fabric. The scrap should be the same or very similar to the fabric you plan to use. Some fabrics retain marking more stubbornly than others, and some do not accept it at all. If you are working with a fabric that you do not intend to wash, you may enlist your friendly neighborhood dry cleaner to help you run tests to see that the marking is removable.

There is a last-resort system of marking on fabrics such as velveteen where the surface is not flat enough to retain pencil, carbon, or iron-on. Choose thin tissue paper for your first tracing. Baste it in place on the surface of the fabric. Mark with basted lines in ordinary sewing thread through both tissue and fabric. Tear away the tissue. You may not have to trace every line, just enough of the major ones to act as guides.

Trace the lines for appliqué on the wrong side of the fabrics. If you need a placement guide, trace them very lightly on the background fabric also.

Stitches

NEEDLEPOINT

Before you start stitching on your canvas, you should bind the edge of it to prevent raveling or snagging. You can do this with masking tape or bias binding.

Don't work with too long a piece of yarn—about 20 inches at a time is enough—or 40 inches doubled. Long pieces are known as "lazy man's thread" and, like many lazy habits, make more problems than they are worth.

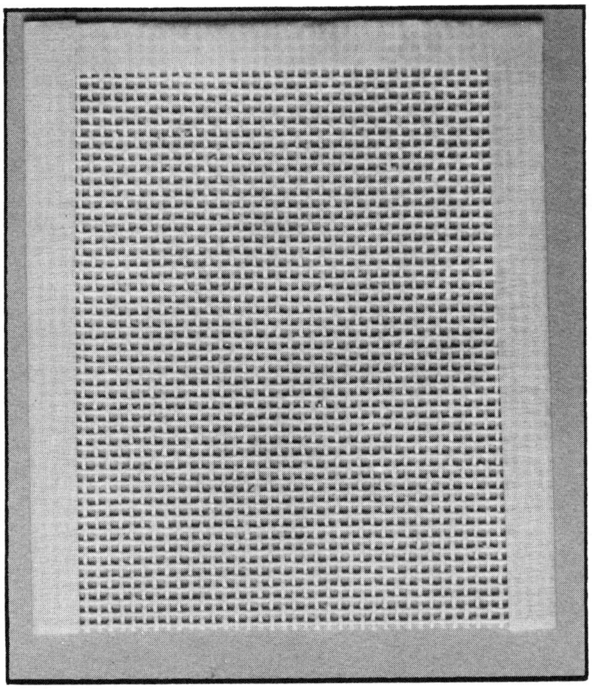

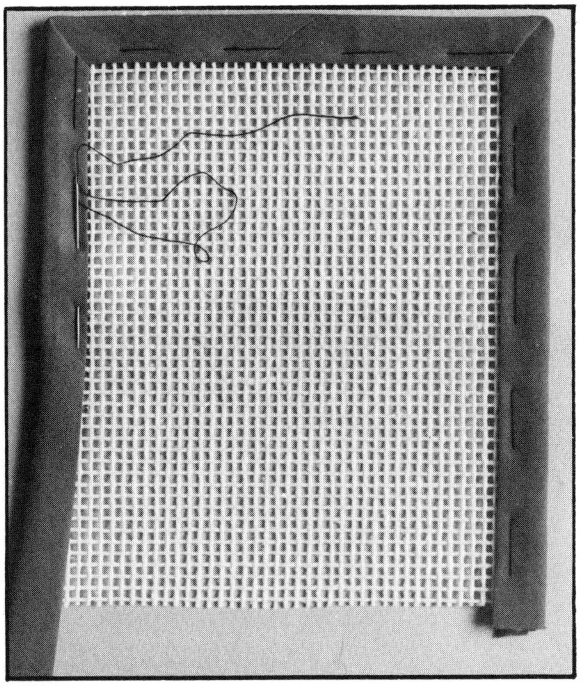

The basic needlepoint stitch is the tent stitch, worked in any one of three ways to give the same surface stitch, but not necessarily the same effect. The half-cross, as shown in the beginning of cross-stitch or counted-thread work, page 21, is really very impractical on needlepoint canvas and should be used only when absolutely necessary to fill in one or two stitches. Large areas can be worked in basketweave or continental stitch, depending somewhat on the shape of the area.

Practice both stitches before starting your canvas. Fill a 1-inch square and keep track of the amount of yarn required so that you can estimate the total amount for each color on the canvas by the number of square inches. Never skimp.

When you start either stitch, bring your needle up through the canvas and hold an inch or two of yarn on the back. Make sure that the stitches are worked over this end to hold it in place. When you finish, work the final end of yarn in under the stitches on the back of the canvas.

The basketweave is best for all large areas and background because it does not warp or pull the canvas out of shape as much as continental. It does take slightly more thread, but it is worth it. Start the basketweave in the upper right-hand corner. You will be working in diagonal rows, each row having one more stitch than the row before, if you are working in a square. The back side is the basketweave; the front is the standard slanted tent stitch. Once you get the hang of it, you will be able to work it in areas of any shape, as well as in large backgrounds.

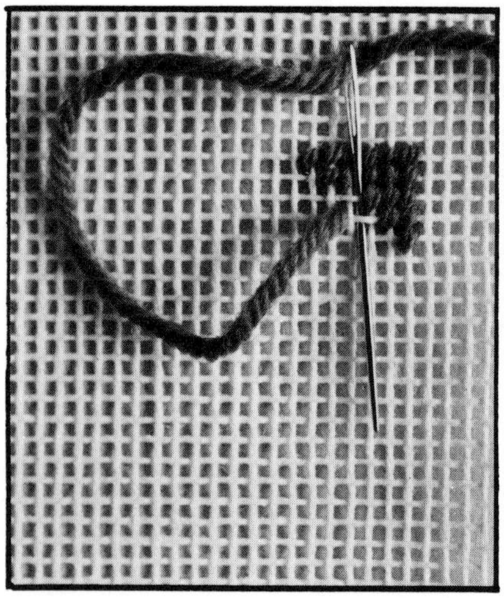

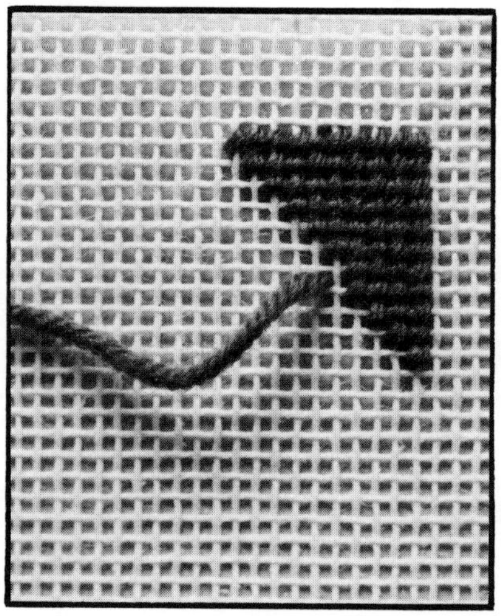

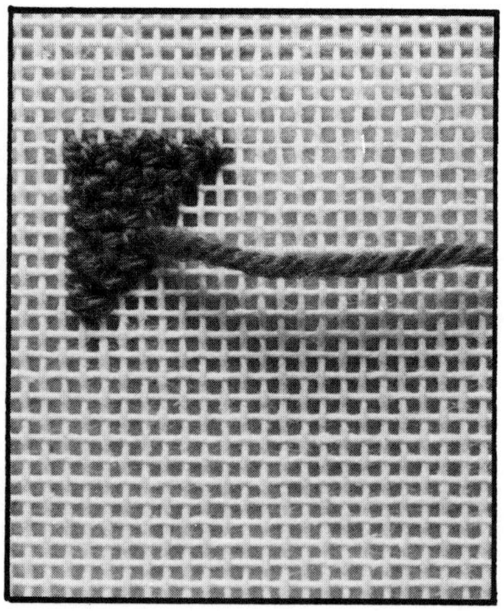

Back view

The continental stitch progresses along a line from right to left, though the stitch itself is carried from left to right on the surface. If you have to work several long rows of continental, start back at the right end for each one, rather than turning around and working back. This method keeps the finished effect smoother.

When you have a single diagonal row of stitches running in the direction opposite the slant of the stitches, you may like the more connected effect gained by crossing these stitches. The larger the canvas, the more necessary this is—see the bag, Plate 2. Only one strand of yarn was used for the crossing, though the rest of the canvas was worked in double yarn.

There are some fine lines and details that do not translate well into needlepoint and so have been worked in backstitch or chain stitch—see Plate 7. This is done after all the needlepoint, including background, is completed.

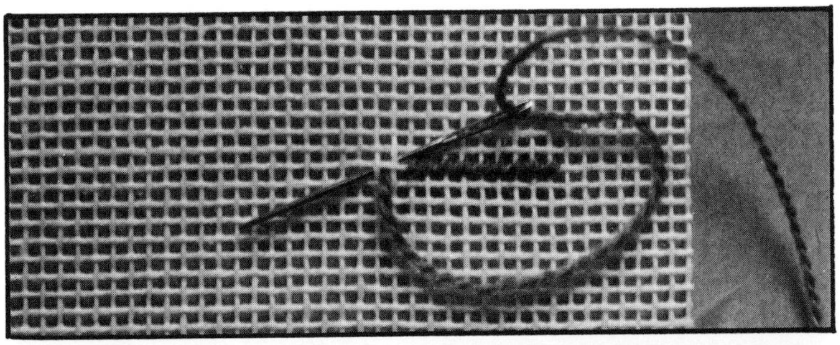

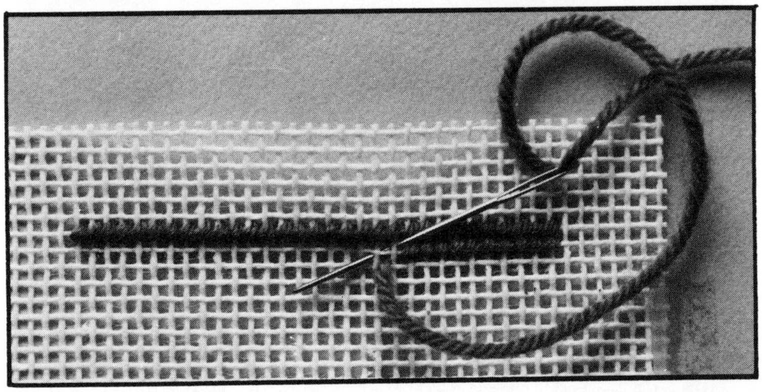

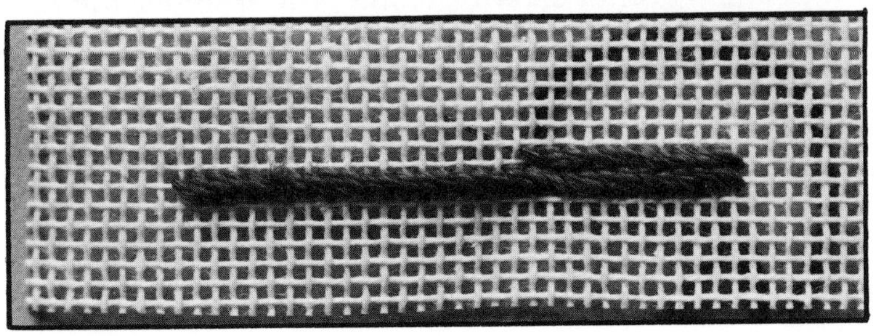

Back view

STITCHERY

Only the simplest of stitches are used in this book, quite effectively, but you may feel free to add to them any others that might enhance your boat. Before beginning on your actual embroidery, experiment with stitches, threads, and yarns, page 4. Even for samples, work with the fabric stretched firmly in a frame or hoop.

Do not tie a knot in the end of the thread. Start by running the needle down through the fabric, out of the way of the design, and leaving a 3-inch end on the surface of the fabric. When you are through working with that entire length of thread, fasten off the final end under the stitches on the back. Pull the first 3-inch piece through to the back, thread it into the needle, and fasten off in the same way.

OUTLINE OR STEM: Makes a nice definite line.

Start by bringing the needle up through the fabric at the left end of the line. Move the needle less than 1/4 inch to the right, insert it into the fabric on the line, and bring it out again on the line about one-third of the way back to where you started. Hold the thread either continuously above or continuously below the needle at every stitch; do not alternate. Keep the stitches very even in length.

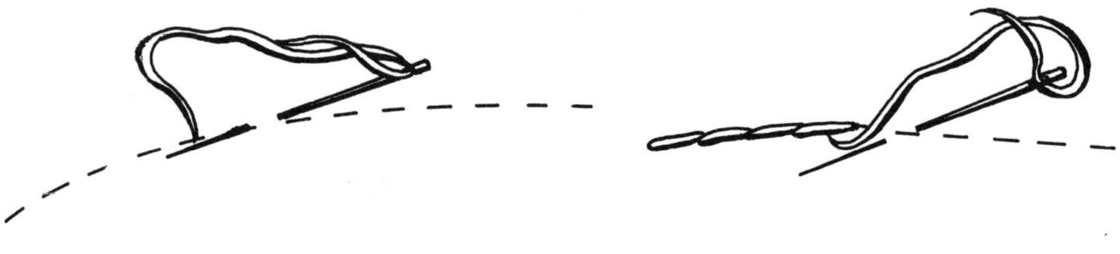

BACKSTITCH: Makes a slightly thinner line than outline.

Bring the needle up less than 1/4 inch from the right end of the line. Put it in again at that end of the line, run it under the fabric and up again less than 1/4 inch from the first stitch. Put it in again at the

first stitch so that the line is completely connected and all stitches on the surface are the same length.

CHAIN: Makes a firmer and more definite line than outline and a very good filler.

Bring the needle up through the fabric at the right end of the line. Throw the thread around in a loop and hold it on the line with your left thumb. Insert the needle at the place where you brought it up. Bring it up again less than ¼ inch along the line and through the loop of thread. Pull the thread, but not too tightly, so that the loop is held in place. Insert the needle through the loop and fabric, and make a second loop or chain along the line exactly like the first one. At the end of the line insert the needle into the fabric just outside the last loop to secure it.

To work chain as a filler, start on the outside outline of the area to be filled. Work successive lines inside that line, touching but not too closely, until the area is filled smoothly.

LAZY DAISY: Single chain stitches used as leaves or flower petals, a charming filler when used as in the Sailfish, Plate 1.

Bring the needle up through the fabric, hold the thread in a loop, and insert the needle at the place where you brought it up. Secure the loop by making a small stitch over the end as in the final chain stitch.

SATIN: Used as a solid filler.

Bring the needle up through the fabric on one edge of the area to be filled. Cross over, straight or diagonally, and insert the needle on the opposite edge. Bring it out very close to the first place on the line and make another stitch across, parallel to the first one. If you feel that the edges of your satin stitch look rough, work around the area with a very fine chain or outline stitch.

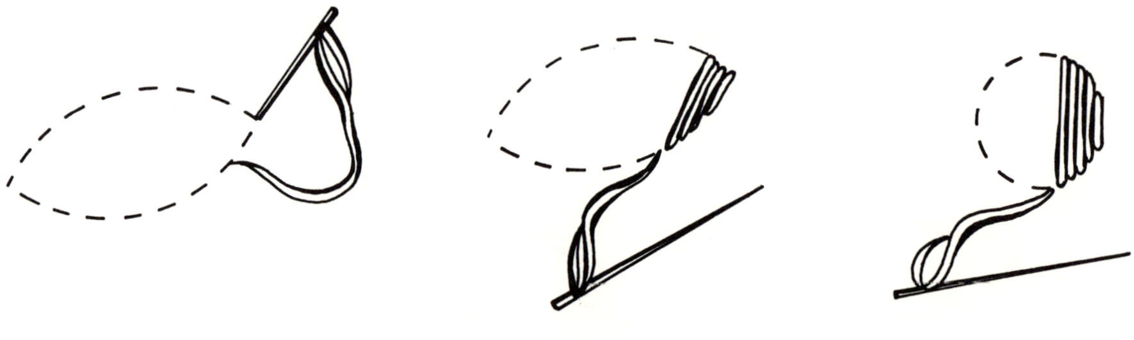

STRAIGHT STITCH OR SEED STITCH: These single straight stitches have many uses, including filling.

Straight stitch is exactly what it sounds like, one straight stitch of any length on the surface of the fabric. When made very small and scattered in many directions to fill an area, it is called seed stitch.

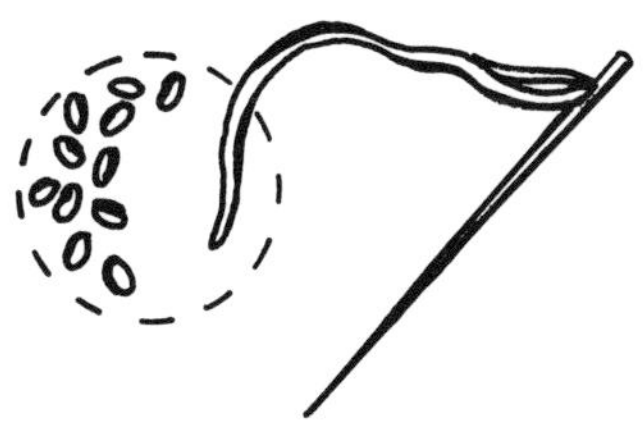

COUCHING AND LATTICE: A way of securing threads to the surface of the fabric, in single rows or crossed as a lattice filler.

The thread that is being laid along the line must be heavy enough to define the line well. The couching thread is finer, so as to be almost invisible, except in lattice when you may want a two-color effect. Lay the heavier thread along the line, bringing it up at one end of the line and down through the fabric at the other end. When all lines are covered, use the finer thread to make little up-and-over stitches about 1/4 inch apart to hold the thread in place. For lattice filler make the securing stitch over the corner intersections.

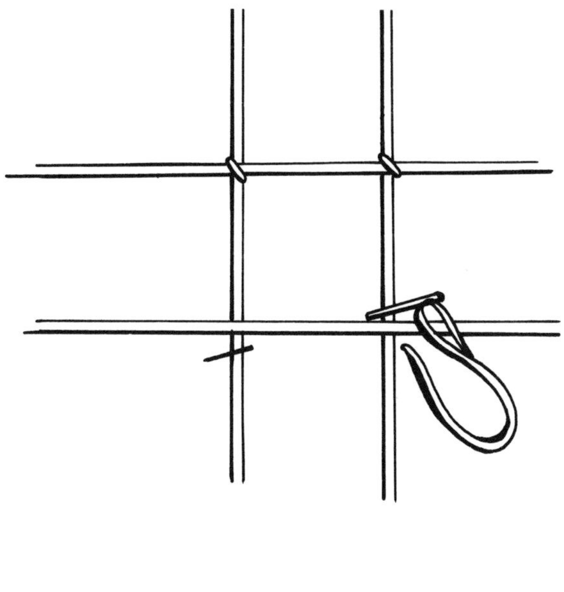

FRENCH KNOT: Used singly for detail and in groups as a filler.

Bring the needle up through the fabric exactly where you want the French knot. Wrap the thread once or twice around the needle, as close as possible to the fabric, insert the needle into the fabric very close to the place it came out, and pull the thread through until the knot is secured on the surface. As a filler, French knots may be scattered, or placed very close together.

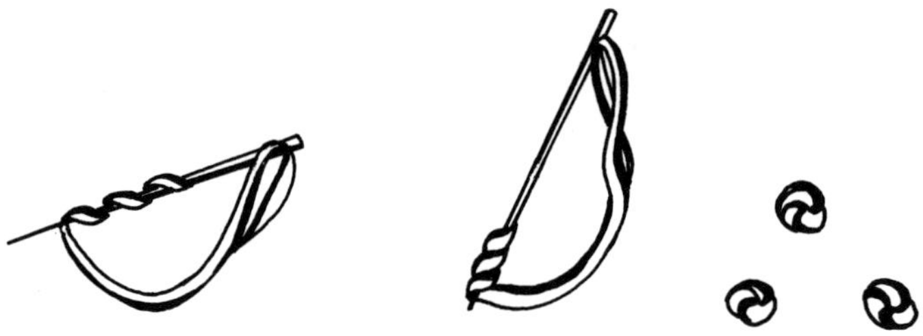

CROSS-STITCH OR COUNTED-THREAD WORK: A versatile stitch that may be used to form an entire design in the same graphed patterns as needlepoint. It may be worked by counting threads, on French canvas, or on perforated paper.

Think of each stitch as a small square. One slanted tent stitch will go from the lower left to the upper right corner and the other one from lower right to upper left. Work several rows of stitches one way, then cross them back.

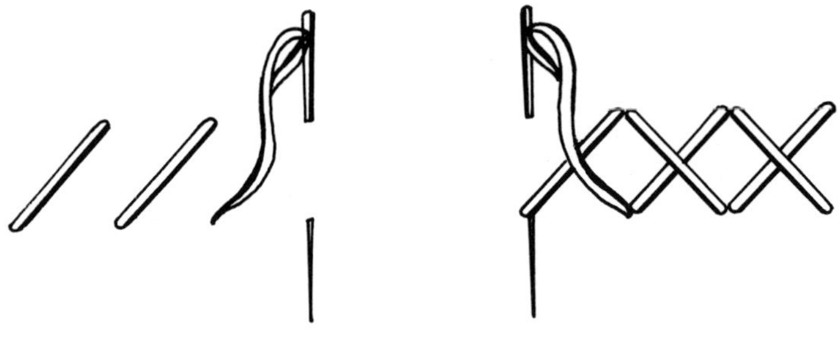

On even-weave fabric, the squares are formed by three threads one way and three the other, or four threads, or however many you want. A truly even weave and good eyesight are necessities.

In using French canvas you can mark the thread intersections for stitches as you can for needlepoint. Baste the canvas onto the fabric. Work the cross-stitches as before, in rows slanting in one direction, then crossing back. Before removing the canvas, soak it or press it with a damp cloth to soften the threads. Remove the basting, ravel the edges of the canvas, and then pull the remaining threads out, one at a time.

Work perforated paper exactly as you do canvas, but remember that it is possible to tear it. To prevent this, put the needle down through the hole, draw the thread through, then up through the next hole, and draw the thread through. Don't try to slip the needle down, under, and up in one stroke.

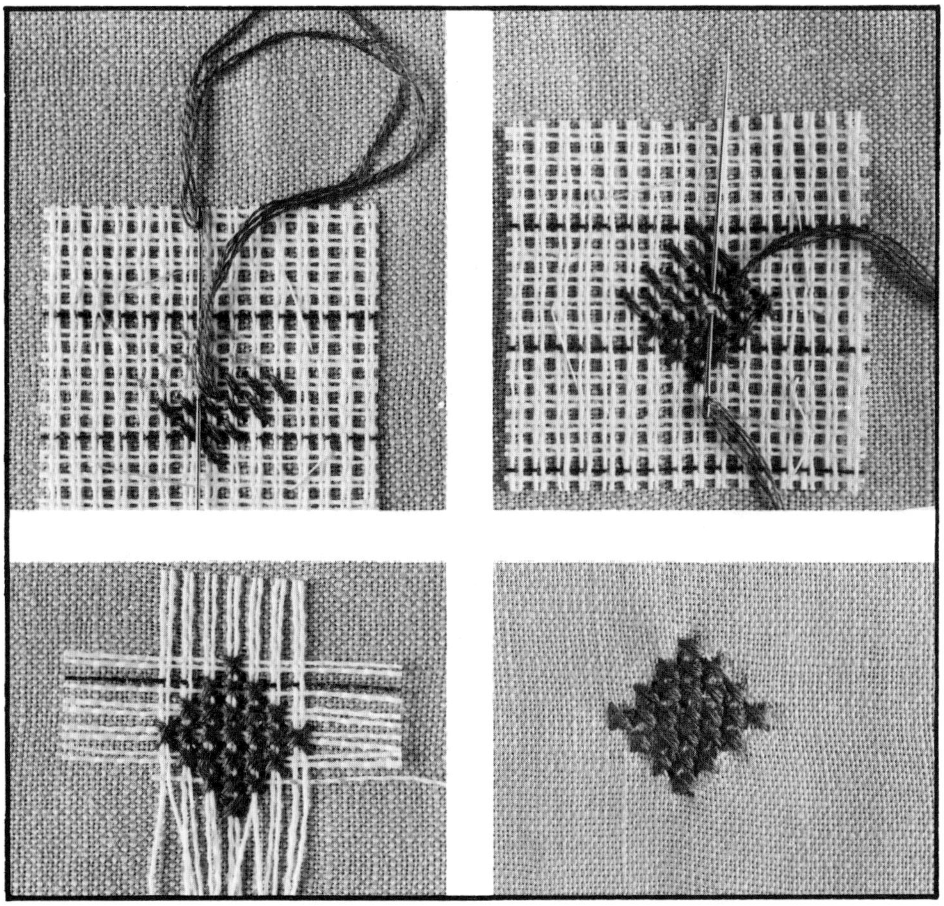

APPLIQUÉ

To achieve a lot of happy colorful effect on quilts, hangings, and clothes, work your designs in appliqué. It can be done by hand, on a zigzag machine (see your machine manual), or even with felt and glue, Plate 3. To make appliqué as simple and effective as possible, enlarge the designs, simplify the lines, and add the little necessary details in stitchery.

Trace the design piece on the wrong side of the appliqué fabric, using the carbon or light-box methods, page 10. Cut a scant 1/4 inch outside the line to allow for seam. As you turn the edge or seam allowance under and baste or press it, you will need to clip the concave curves and corners and notch out small wedges from the convex ones.

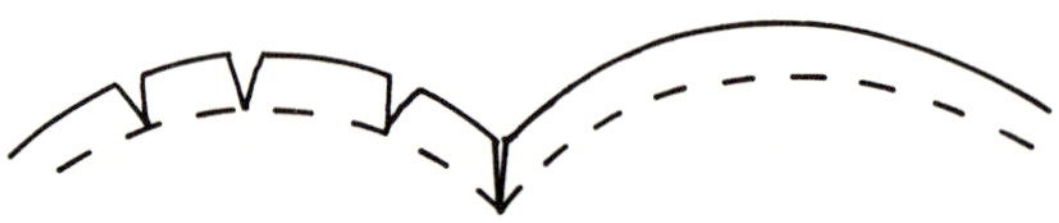

When the appliqué pieces are prepared with edges turned, place them on the background fabric and pin or baste them in place. You will find that the various pieces should be laid on in a logical order, with some turned edges overlapping some that are left unturned.

Note: If you have had trouble turning edges smoothly, you may find it useful to run a row of machine or hand stitching along the outline drawn on the wrong side of the fabric. The stitching gives a hard line to the edge and makes it turn more smoothly.

Use ordinary sewing thread and a short needle to sew the edge in place. The proper stitch is called a blind stitch because so little of it shows on the surface. Bring the needle up through the base fabric and through just a thread or two of the turned edge of the appliqué piece. Put the needle back in the base fabric just over the edge; run it under the base fabric for 1/4 inch or less and then up through both fabrics again. Repeat at very even intervals.

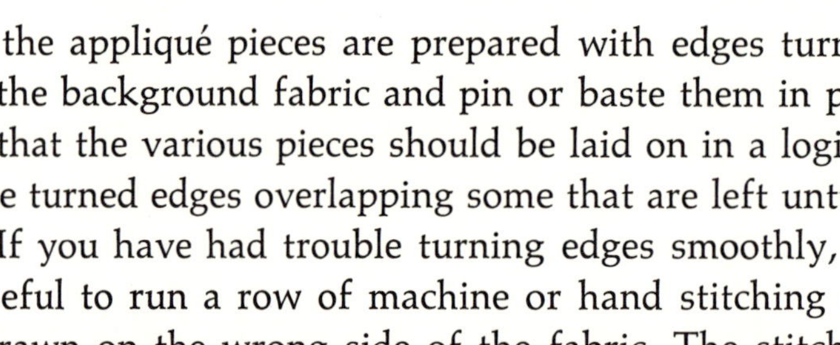

A good trick for narrow pieces like masts and spars is to use folded bias. Cut the bias slightly less than four times the desired finished width of the piece. Fold it in half lengthwise. Use a running stitch to attach it along the line of one edge of the mast or spar, with about two-fifths of the piece along the raw edge covering the placement area and the other three-fifths along the folded edge lying away from the placement area. Now, fold the piece over, covering the raw edges entirely, and blind stitch the folded edge along the other placement line.

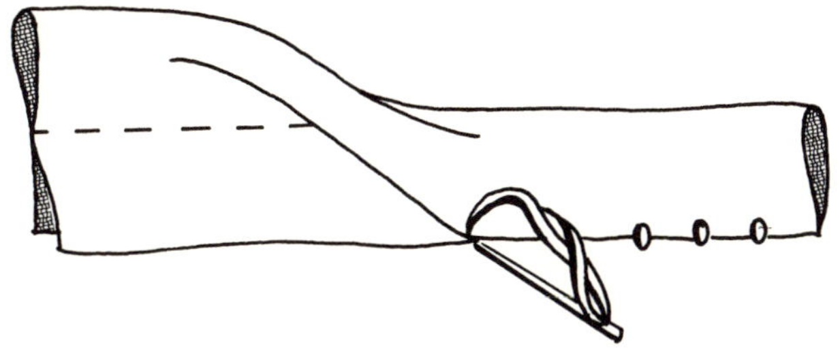

Another useful technique for small areas like windows (see the lighthouse on the cover) is reverse appliqué. Cut out the window hole, allowing very small seams, clip into the corners, and slide a small piece of colored fabric underneath. Turn and baste the edge to the colored piece and through to the background. Blind stitch it in place, working very carefully around the corners.

SPECIAL HELP

If you are a real beginner, seek all the good advice you can get. There are two handy paperback books, also from Charles Scribner's Sons, that reinforce and elaborate on the techniques. They are:

The ABC's of Needlepoint by Hope Hanley

Ask Erica by Erica Wilson

Drawing Your Own Design

You do not have to be Rembrandt to dare to draw an embroidery design from a boat or any other simple object. There are lots of available aids to your efforts if you only take time to assemble them. We started to do a diagram of the S-boat *Cottontail* by finding a good photograph that someone had taken of her in a race. The picture was so nice, with the two extra boats in the background, that we decided to use the whole thing first and then make a close-up of the central boat.

The picture was enlarged to the size we needed, and from that we could trace the main lines. After that there are two important points: play up the predominant feature of the boat, and eliminate unnecessary detail. The most recognizable features of the S-boat are its raked mast and small jib. So the point for our purposes was to be careful not to straighten the mast.

S-Boat

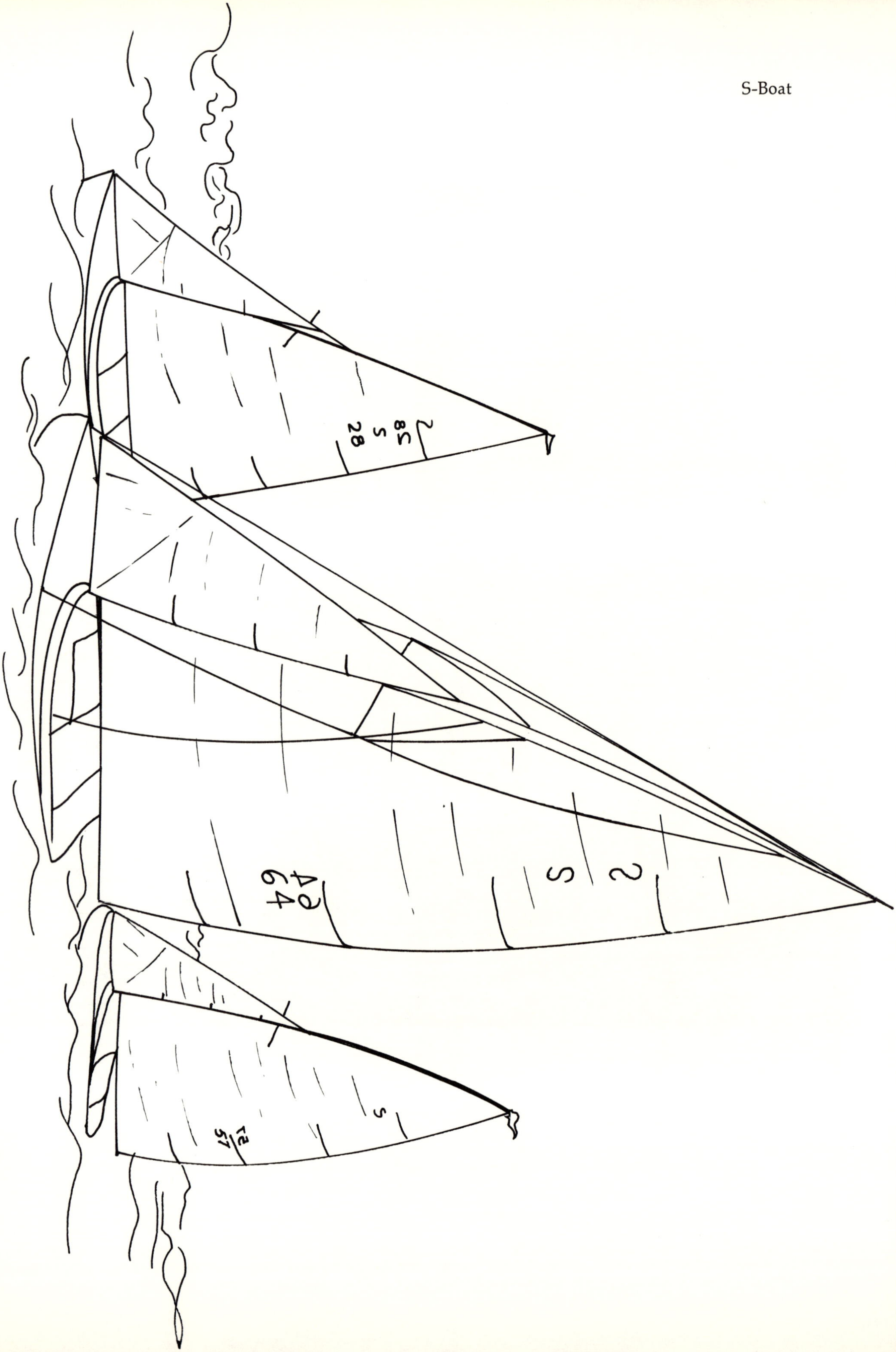

The appliquéd Sailfish is enlarged one and one-half times to fit into an 11-inch block to be used in a quilt. See diagram, page 32.

Only five types of stitches are used to make a colorful stitchery Sailfish and monogram on a blue chambray shirt. See diagram, page 32.

The needlepoint pennant on 18-to-the-inch canvas makes a distinctive marker for duffelbag, sail bag, or any other sea-going articles. See diagrams, pages 83, 85, and 87.

The tote bag for racing aficionados can be made quickly on 5-to-the-inch canvas. The same graph worked on 18-to-the-inch canvas makes a good identification patch. See diagram, page 75.

The U.S. Power Squadron can show its colors in an ensign made of felt and stitched together on a sewing machine. The diagram, page 72, can be enlarged to any size wanted.

The Hudson River Sloop *Clearwater* is on parade on a cloudless, windy day—the kind sailors dream of. The washable polyester felt and machine construction can withstand much worse weather. See page 34.

Plate 4

Tugboats seem sturdy enough to become bedside rugs for small boys. This one is a design drawn from *The C. Hayward Meseck* on a typical overcast day in New York Harbor. See diagrams on pages 37 and 39.

Plate 5

The Compass Rose makes a fine design for a delicate silk bookend. It is all worked in chain stitch in Pearl Cotton. The same diagram, page 76, doubled in size, makes a traditional quilt block.

A plain log book or diary of sailing trips can be covered in silk with the design of the owner's boat worked quickly in chain stitch. See page 64 for the Star diagram.

Drake's Galleon sailed again—into the New World for the Bicentennial Op Sail. It is worked here in Persian yarn and outline stitch on a linen tote bag, doubled in size from the diagram, page 56.

Hobie Cats are built for fun and their most popular sail colors are the ones shown here, called Tequila Sunrise. The design for appliqué or stitchery is on page 58.

Plate 7

Pillows, especially needlepoint ones with designs that hit home, are always welcome gifts. Whatever a person's dreams of boats, one of these must fit.

The *Queen Elizabeth II*, there and back, is a must for anyone who loves ocean voyages. This one is worked on 10-to-the-inch canvas; diagram on page 41.

A fisherman may be using a 10-foot rowboat, but he can dream about a sea-going craft equipped to perfection. The design from pages 43 and 45 is worked on 14-to-the-inch canvas.

A Bristol 40 is the kind of boat that makes both the racing and the cruising members of the family happy. Here it is worked on 14-to-the-inch canvas and trimmed in velveteen, page 47.

Victorian cross-stitch paper and plain notes combine to make very personalized cards, Christmas or otherwise, for sailing friends. The one-design sail insignia diagrams are on pages 67, 68, and 71.

The crew of any racing boat would be sharply fitted out in T-shirts with the craft's insignia and number. Only two types of stitches are used on this Lightning. See diagrams, pages 70 and 88.

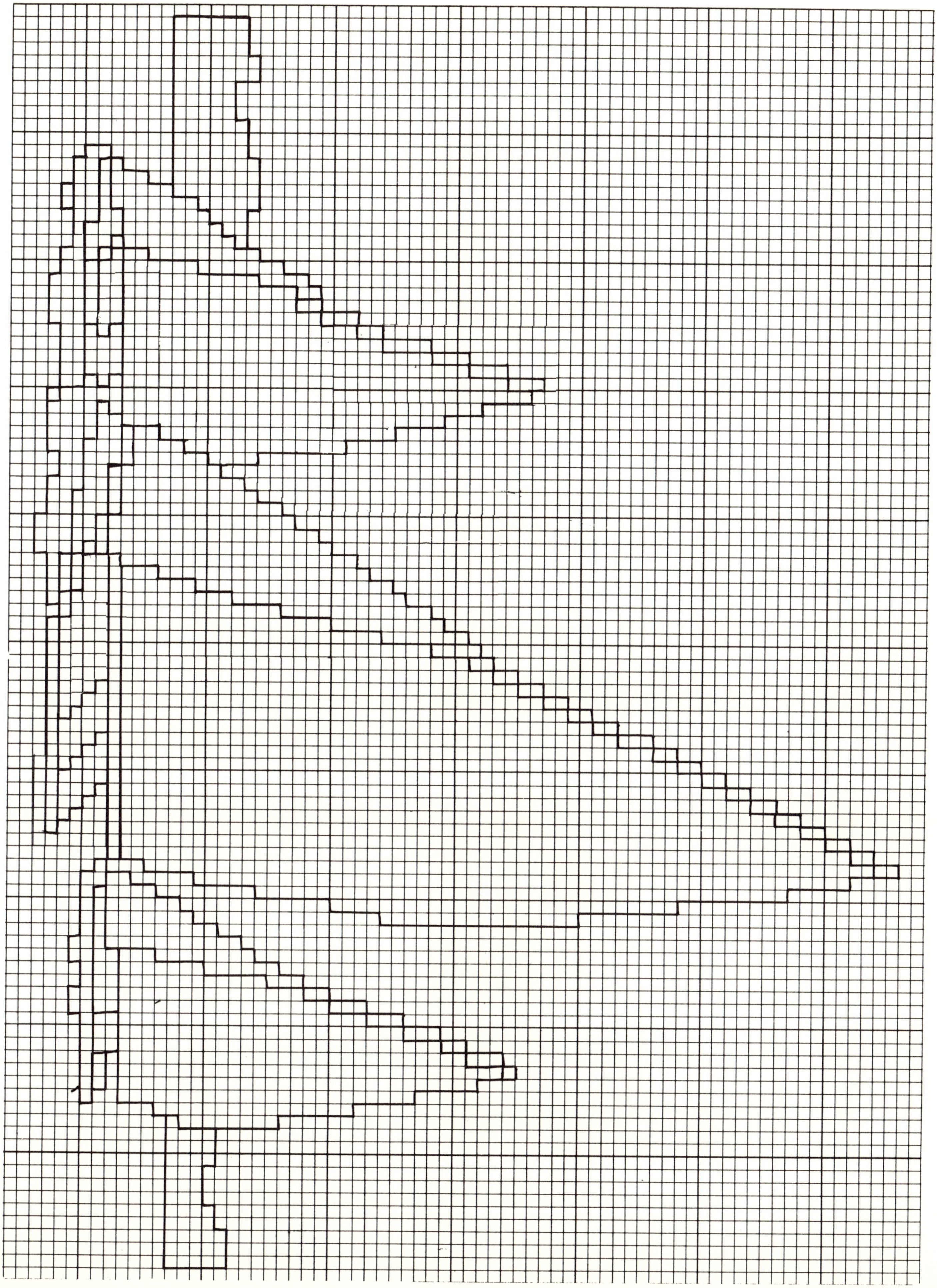

S-Boat

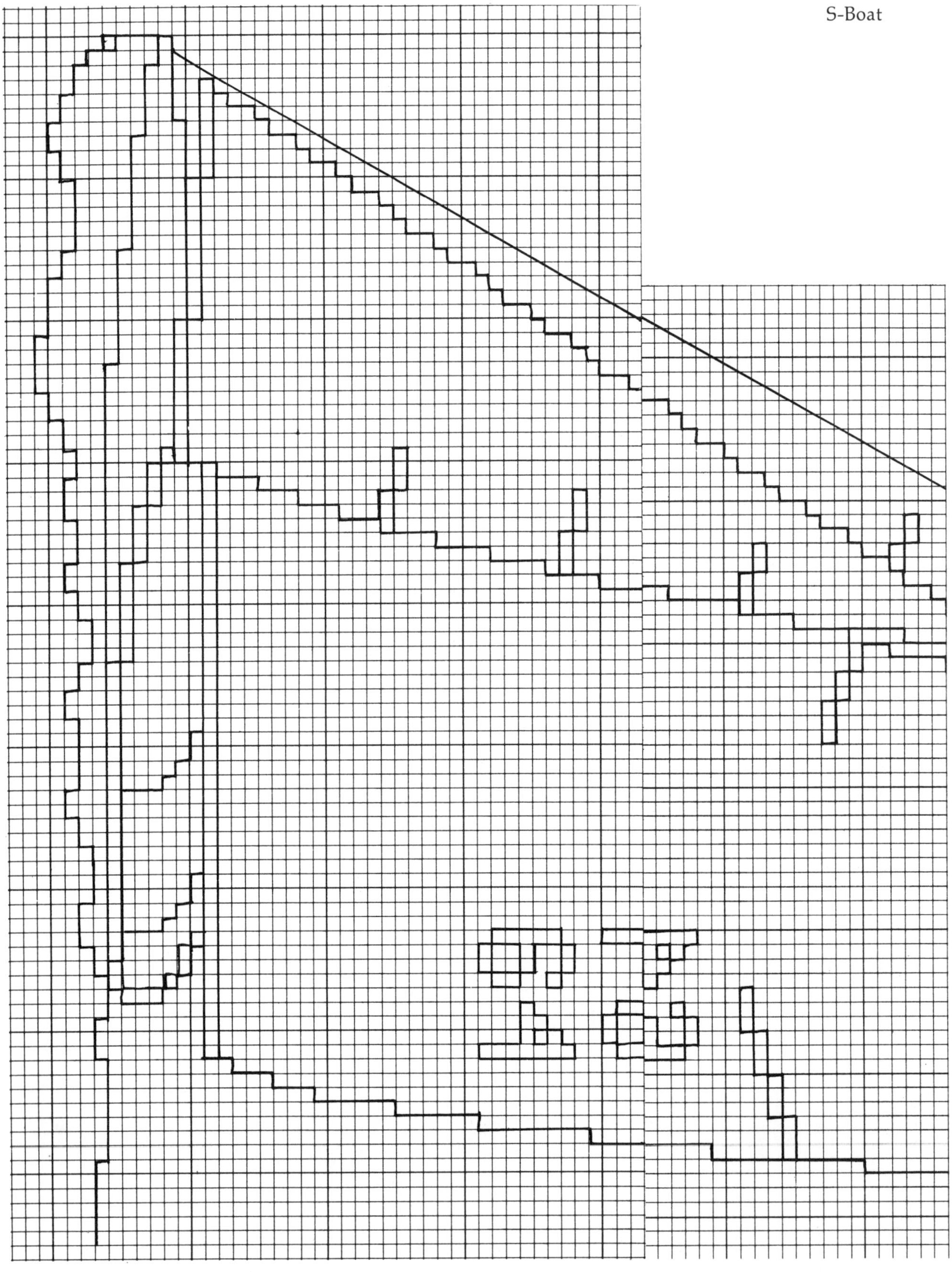

Join

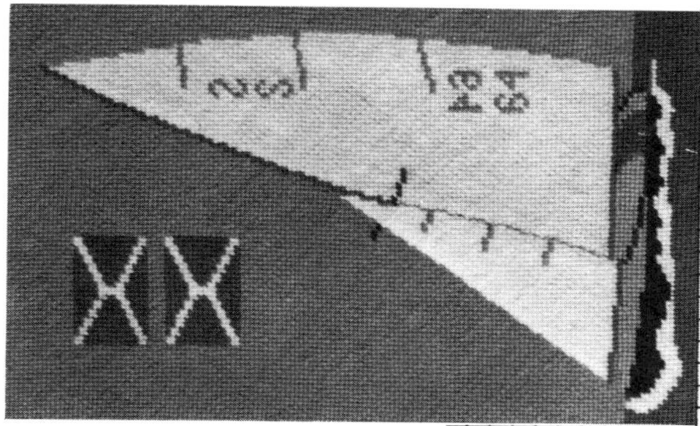

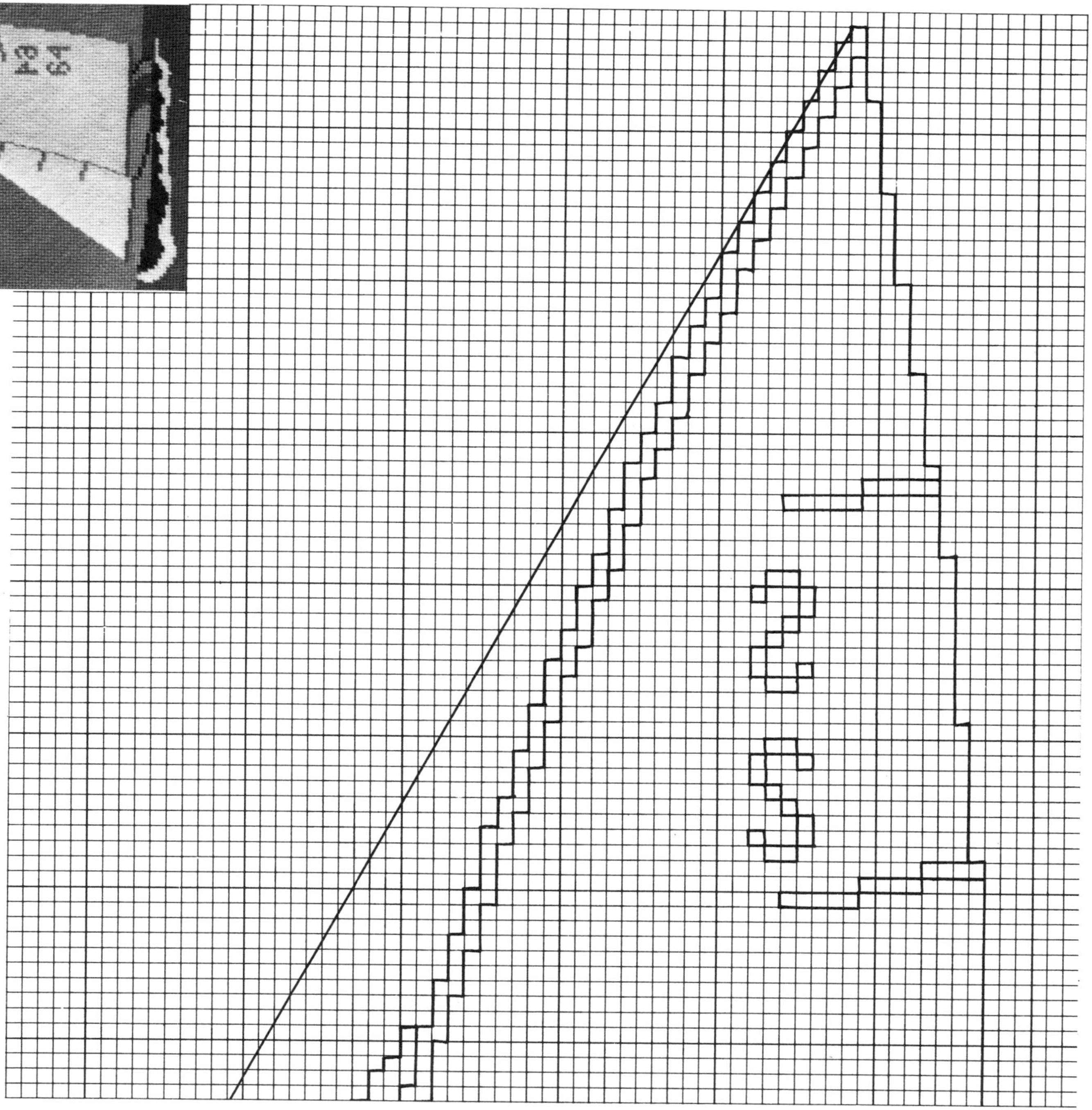

Join

As you look through the boats, you will notice many more such trademarks. The twin hull and often gaudily colored sails say Hobie Cat, even if you can't see the big *H* insignia. The *Queen Elizabeth II* has a long, slim hull design and very distinctive stack. Almost everyone can recognize the lateen rig of the Sailfish and Sunfish, which are seen on every body of water larger than a bathtub. If these familiar features are pointed up in the embroidery design, the message is clear, even though the boat is not represented perfectly in small detail.

Most of the shading in a photograph can be eliminated in favor of clean line for embroidery. The sail panels can be reduced to a few broken lines unless you want them to be a predominant part of the design, as in the Hobie Cat and the 12-Meter's beautiful spinnaker. The lines of the battens should be left in to help define the curve of the sail.

Sometimes it is easier to get a good likeness of a boat by working from a drawing or spec sheet. These are more two-dimensional and therefore shading is totally unnecessary. The entire hull shows in such a drawing and often gives a more interesting proportion. Boat dealers have such drawings available, or you may find them in boating magazines and books.

If you shudder at the thought of scaling a drawing up to the size you want, it may be worth spending a few dollars to have a photostat house do it for you. On page 90 you will find three graphs. If you trace a drawing and lay it over the 1/4-inch graph, then draw the same lines, as you see them in each square, on tissue over one of the larger graphs, you can enlarge a drawing to twice its size (on the 1/2-inch) or three times its size (on the 3/4-inch). It helps to have the graph sheets copied so that they can lie flat on your drawing board.

To convert the designs for use in needlepoint or cross-stitch, use sheets of 1/8-inch graph paper, available at any stationery store. Trace the line design onto the graph paper with carbon and a fine-point pen or hard pencil. With erasable pencil start changing those lines into the nearest corresponding lines of the graph paper.

It's interesting to see how the angles of the lines work into small graph blocks. A 45-degree angle is a stair-step, up one and over one, up one and over one. If the angle changes slightly, you may be able to follow it with up one, over one, up two, over one, up one, over one, and so on. The next change in angle will then be up two, over one, up two, over one. Each of these changes of number allows the line to slant more gradually. In complete circles there is a change at a given point in each quarter—see the emblem for the Chesapeake 20, page 69. Once you've worked out one quarter, the others are simply repeats.

The larger you make the design (the more graph squares that are used for the same picture), the more detail you can get into it. Look at the center boat taken from the picture of the three S-boats and enlarged. It is a far more accurate representation of the boat than the smaller one with the two even smaller ones behind it. Of course, the final size of the worked piece of needlepoint depends on the size of the canvas used. If the larger boat were worked on 18-mesh canvas it would be very nearly the same size as the smaller one worked on 10-mesh.

Remember that effect is what you're working for. Even after you've drawn the design to your satisfaction, you may want to make changes in the actual stitchery. Different stitches and different colors affect the final outcome. Don't be afraid to change your mind. When all else fails, put the embroidery away for a day; then get it out so that you can get a fresh approach, and you may very quickly see what your problem was.

The Patterns

BOATS AND SHIPS

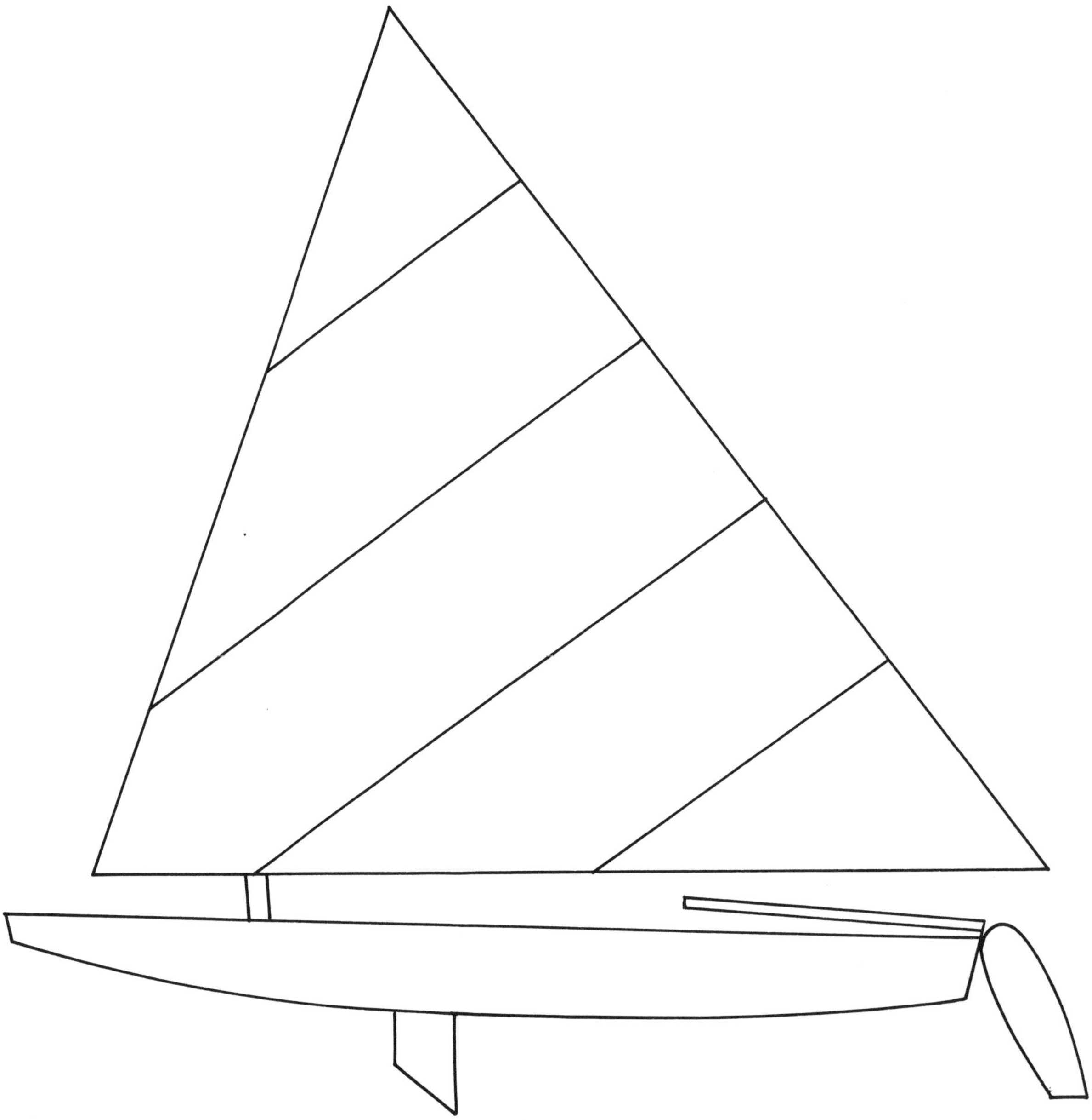

Sailfish *See Plate 1*

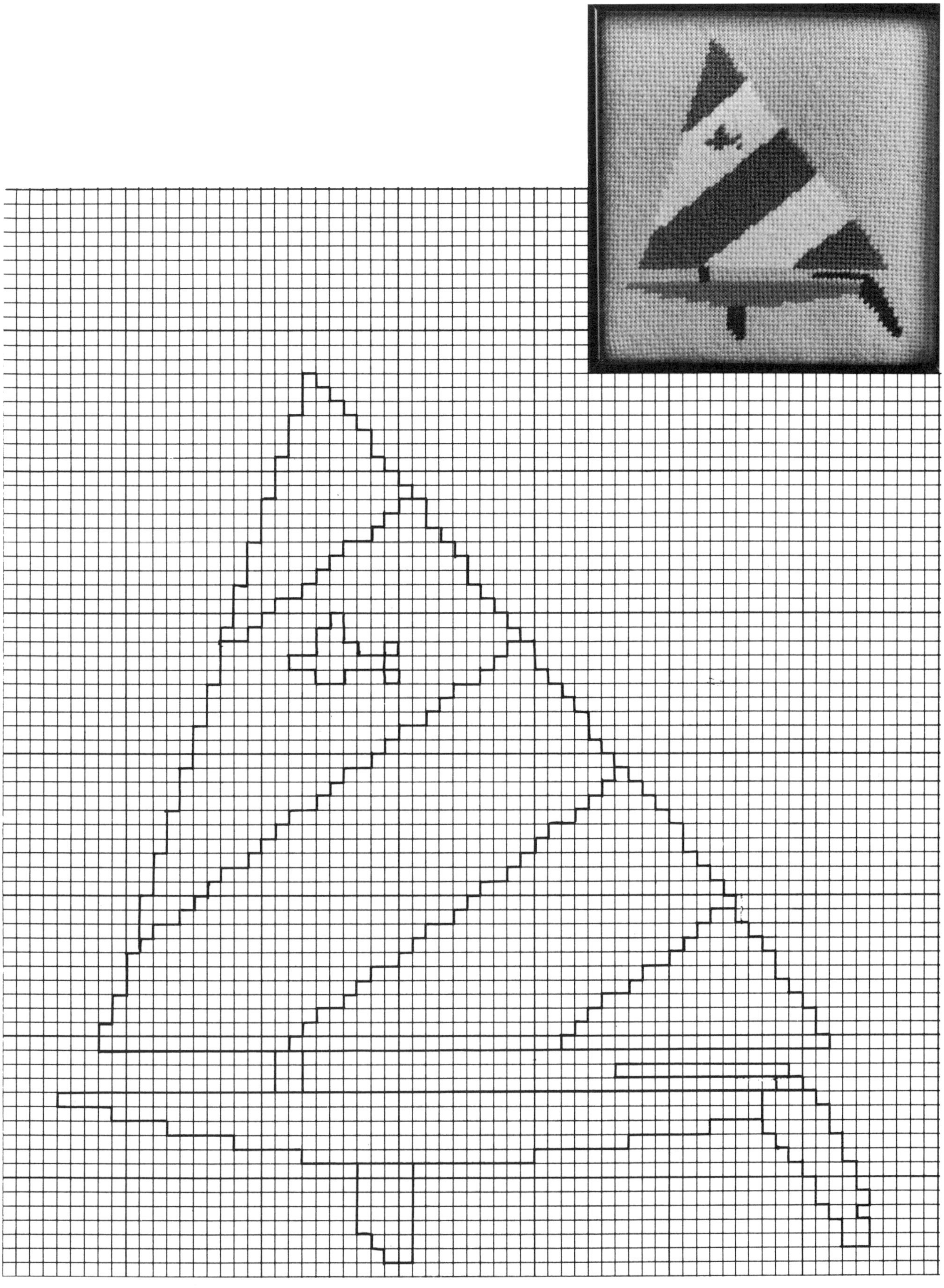

Hudson River Sloop *Clearwater* *See Plate 3*

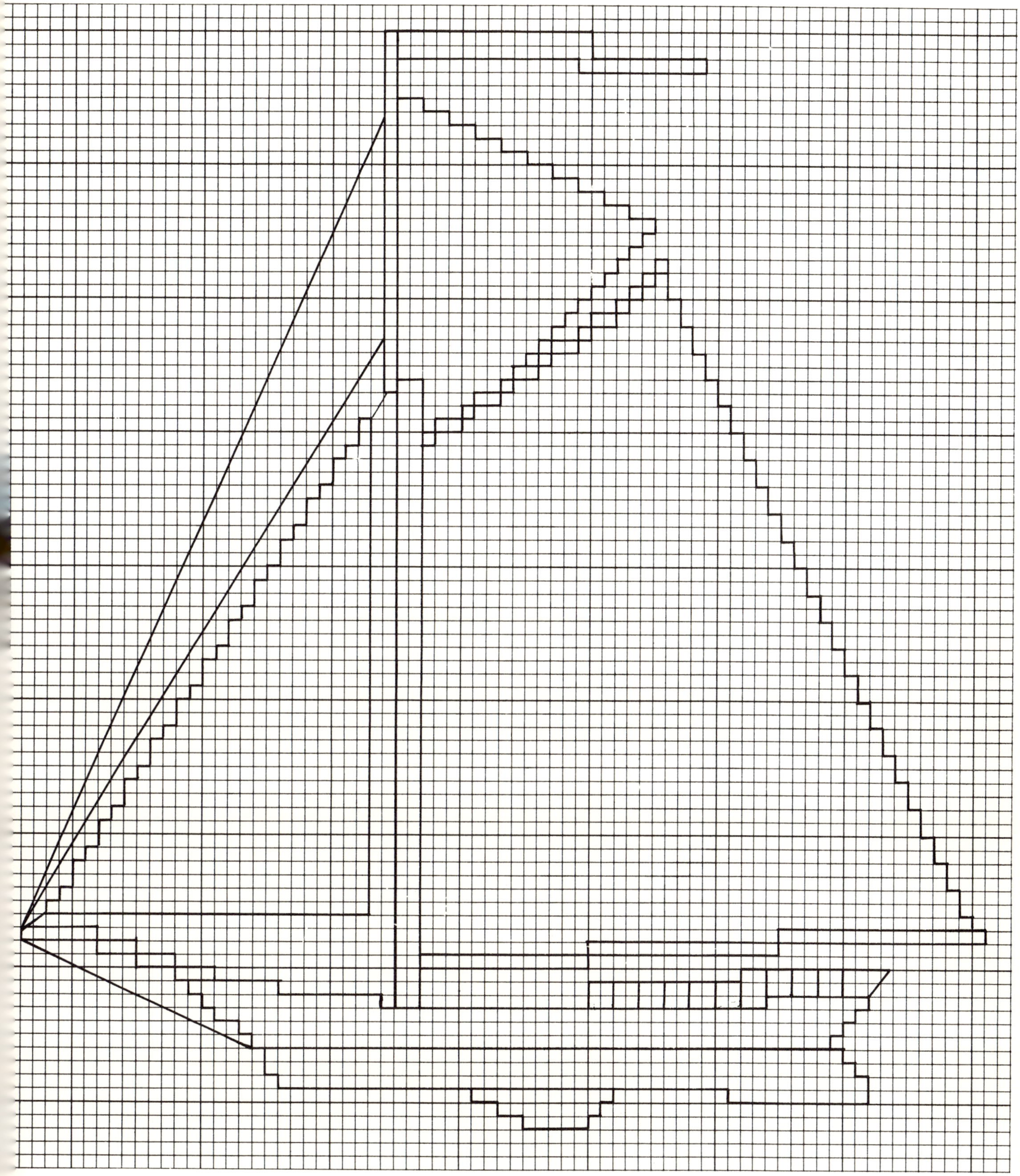

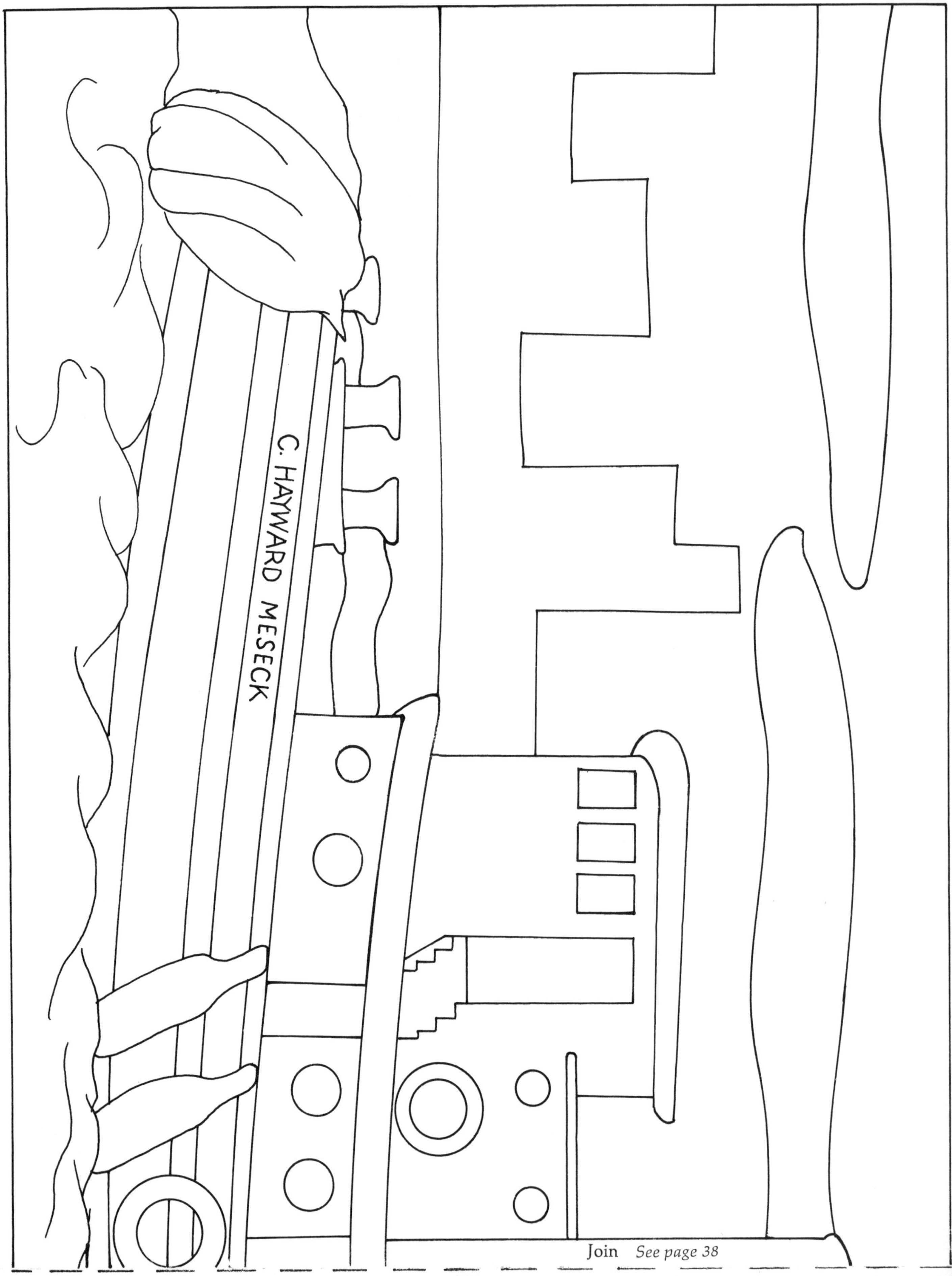

Join *See page 38*

Tugboat

Join *See page 39*

See Plate 4

Join

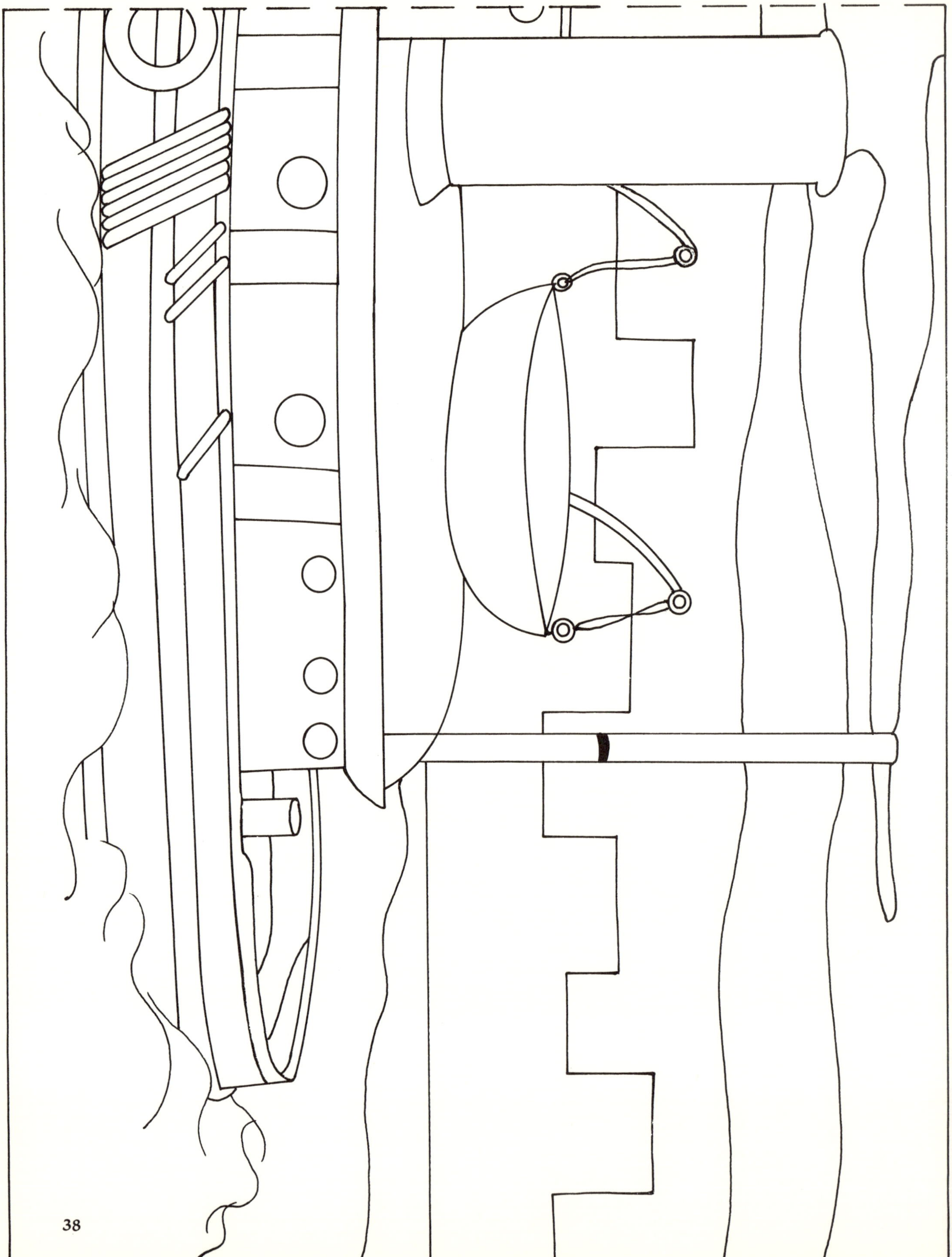

Tugboat

Join

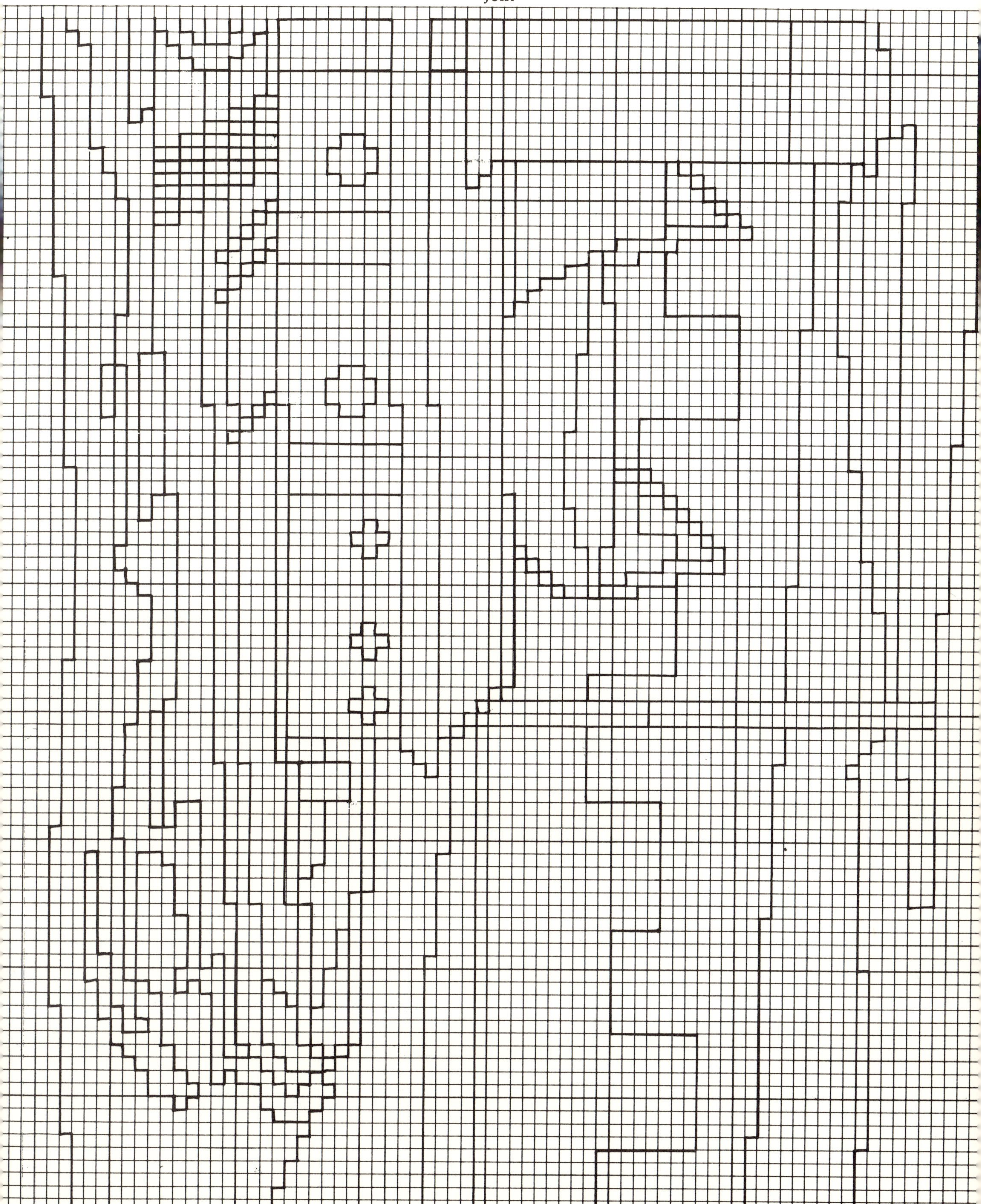

See Plate 4

Join

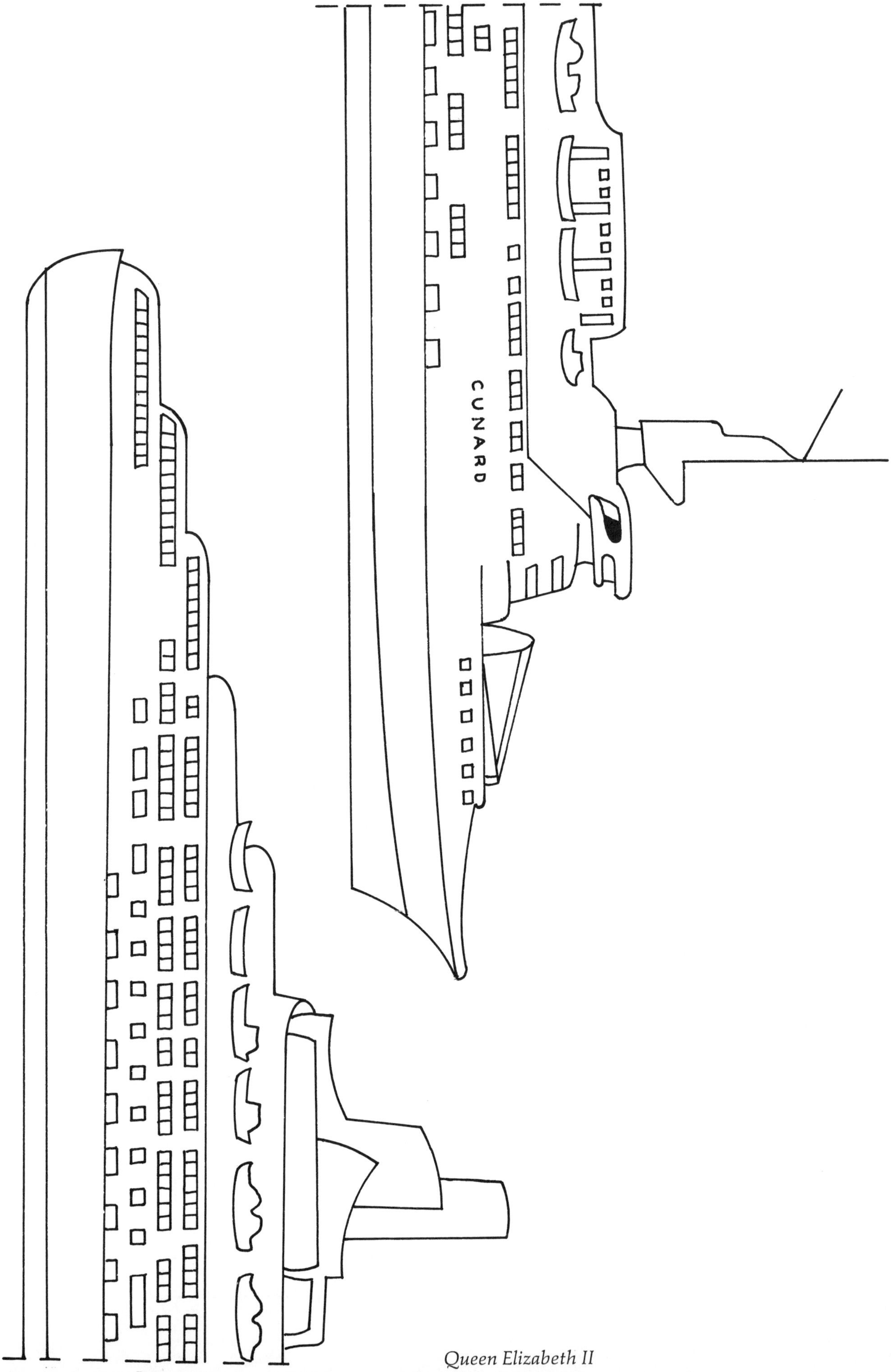

Join

Queen Elizabeth II

Join

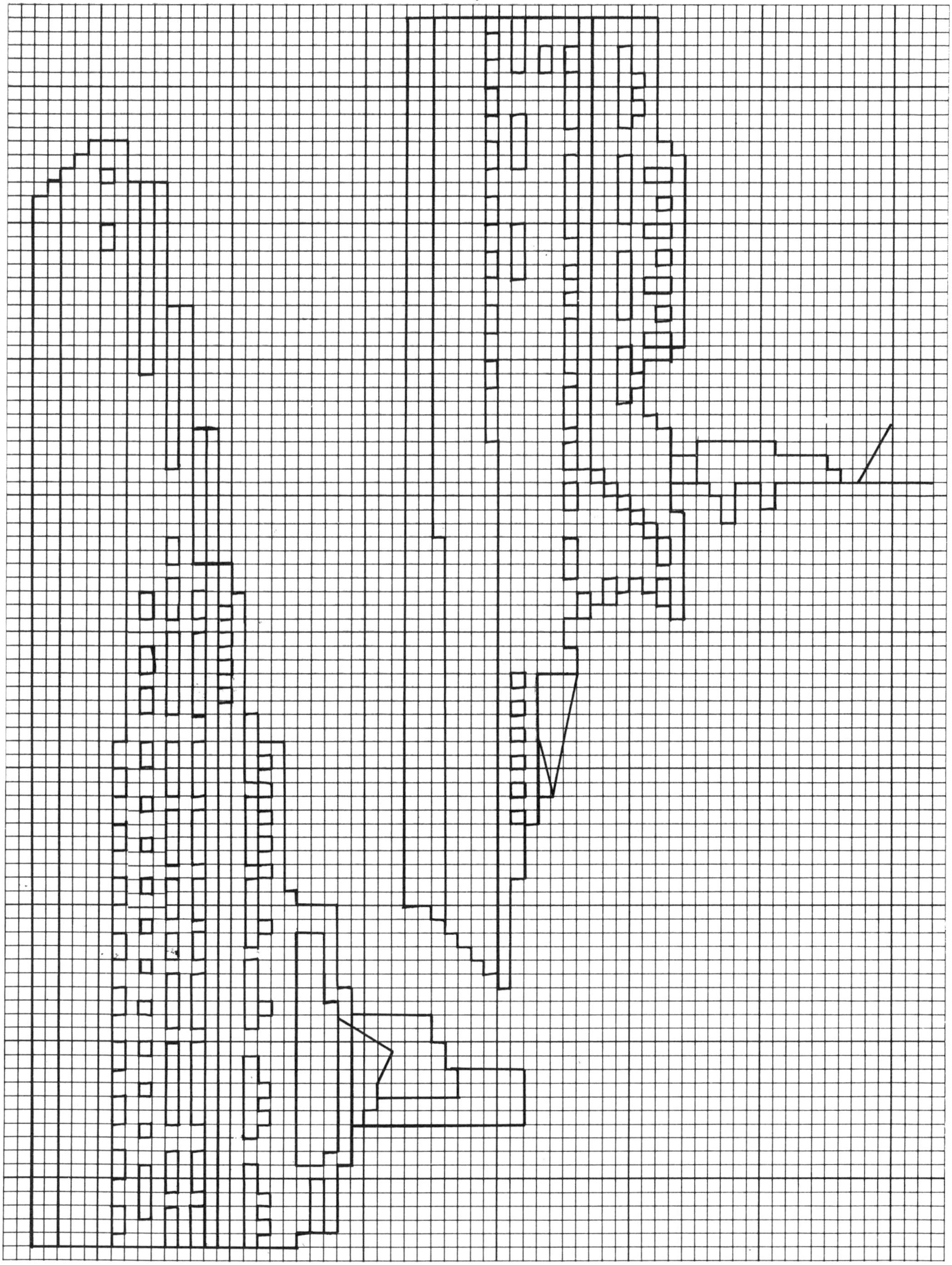

Join

See Plate 7

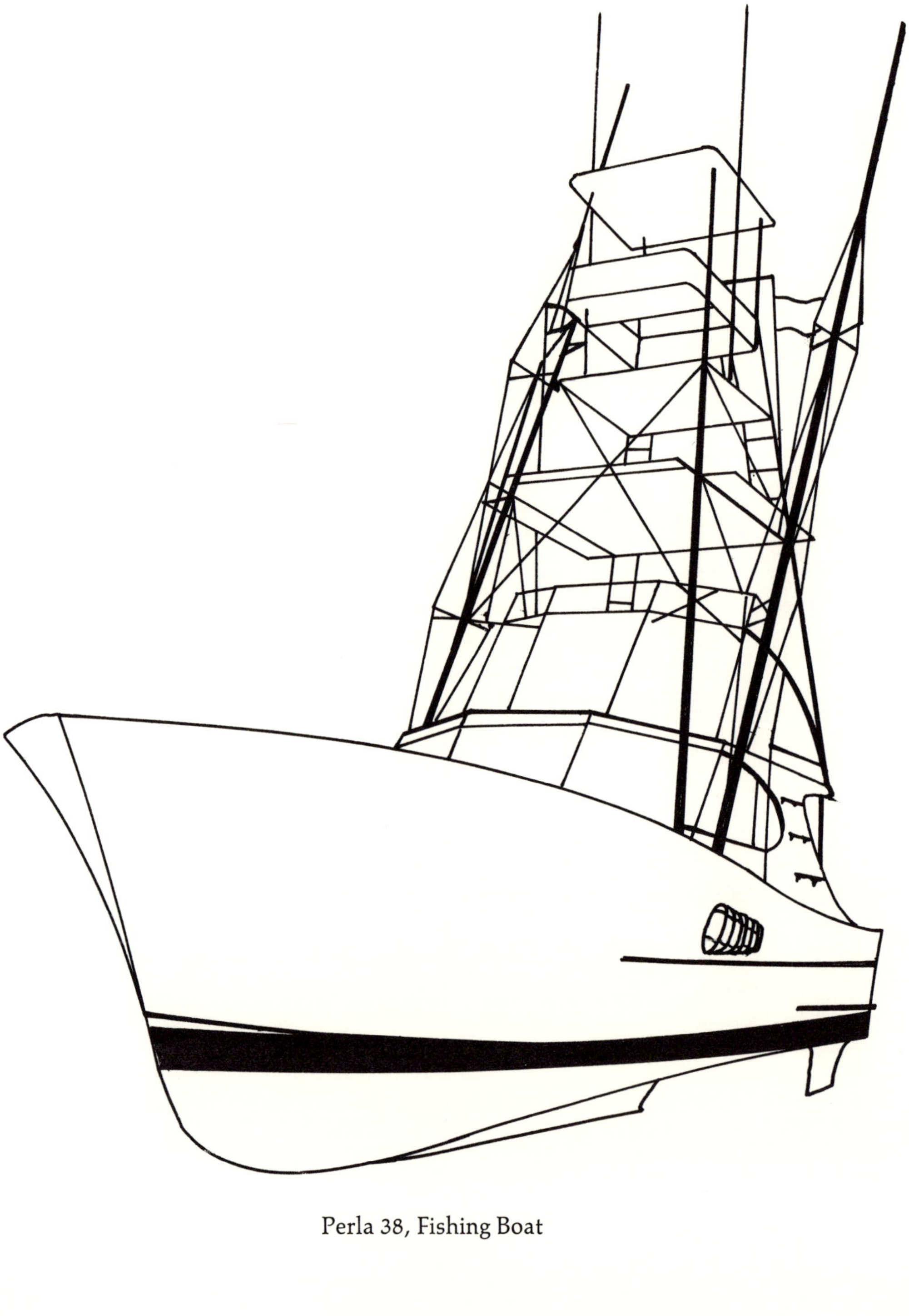

Perla 38, Fishing Boat

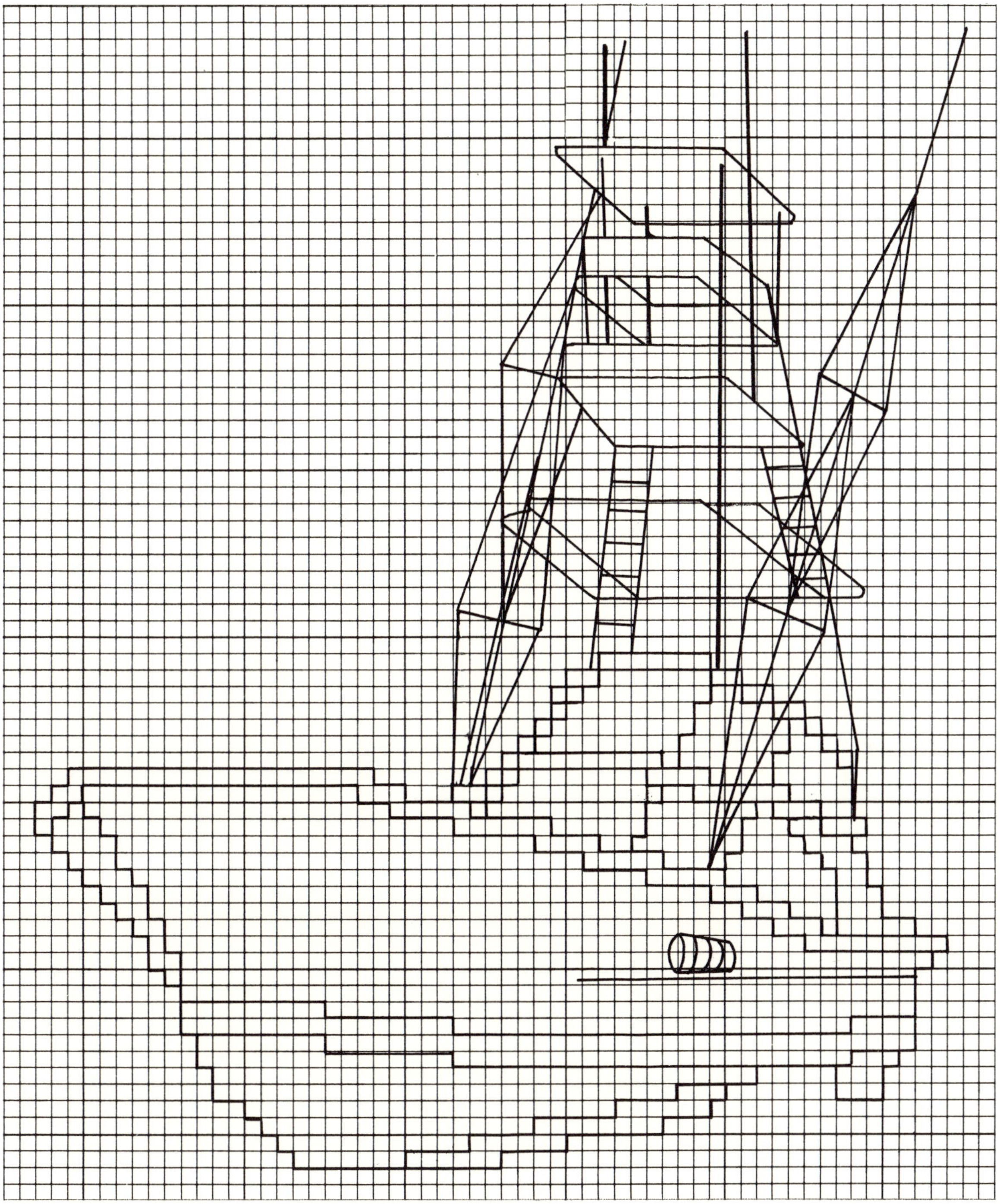

See Plate 7

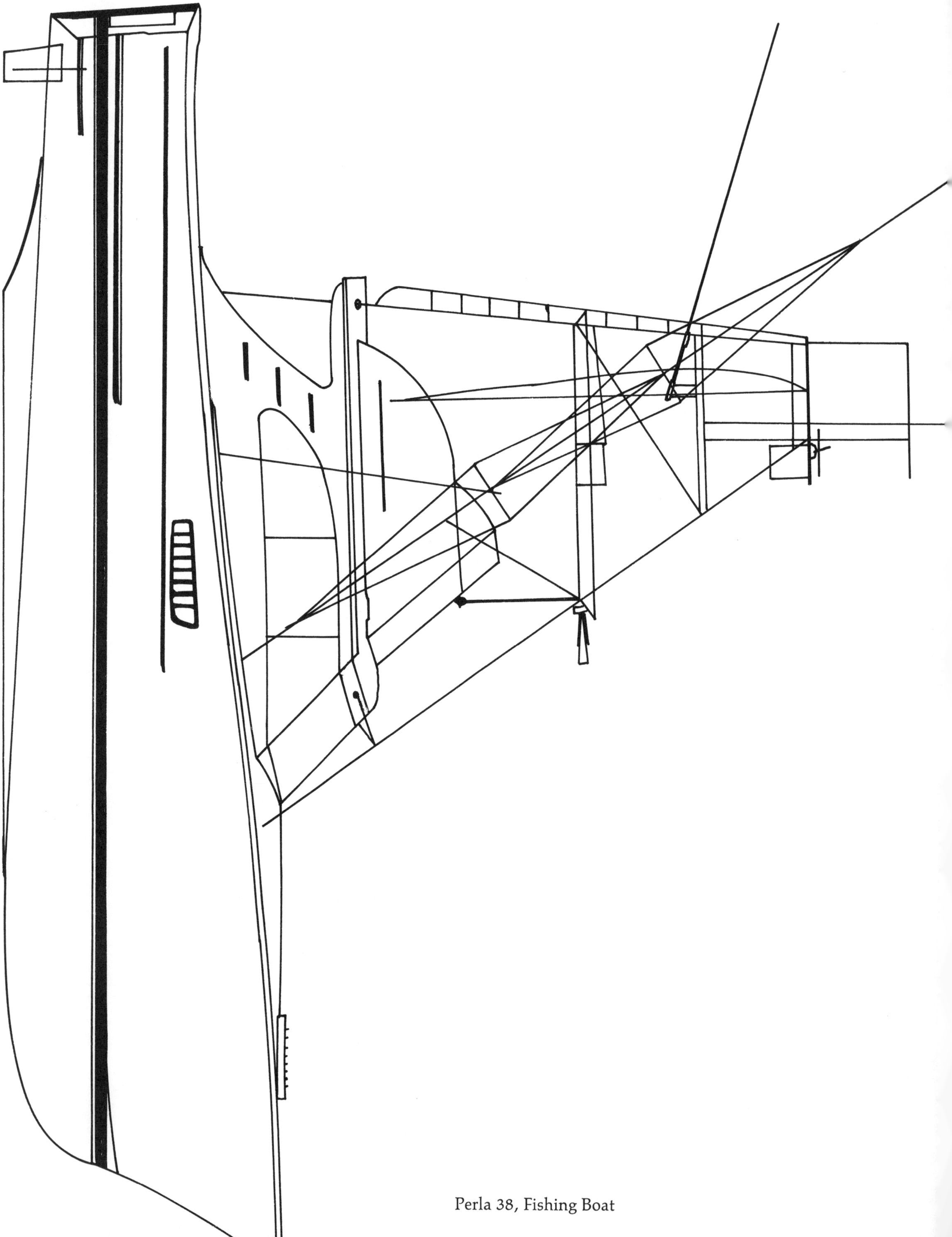

Perla 38, Fishing Boat

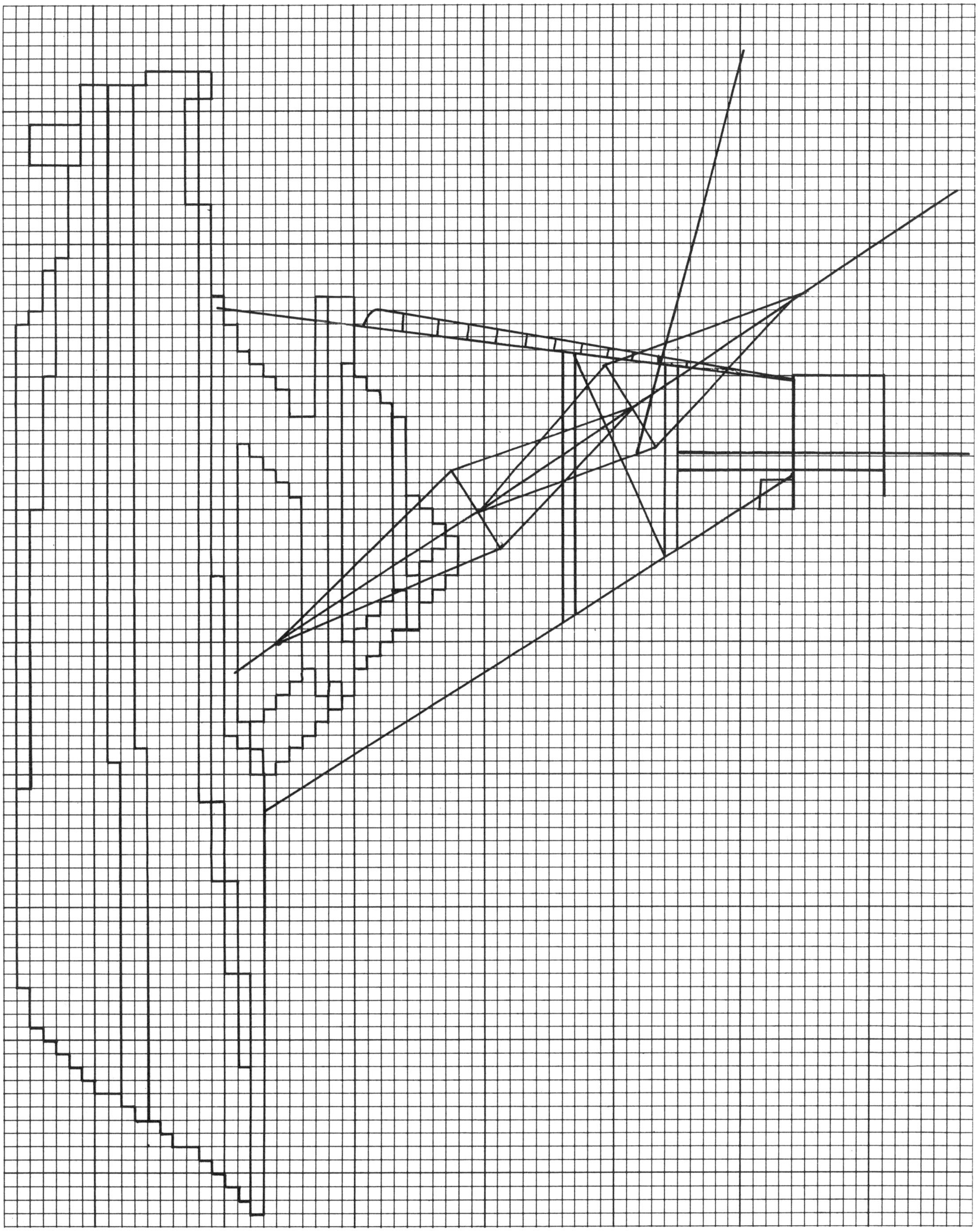

See Plate 7

Bristol 40, Racing-Cruising Boat

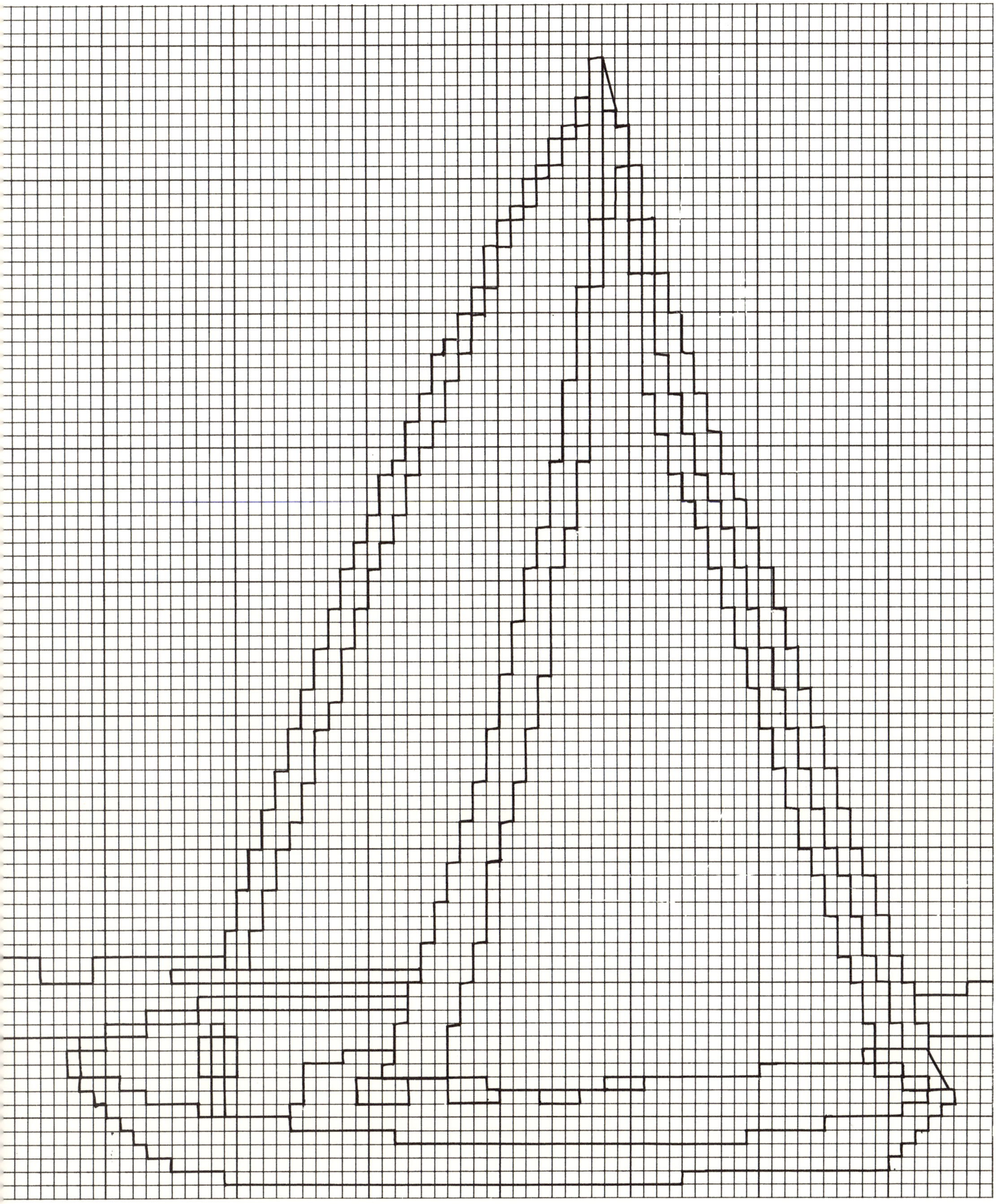

See Plate 7

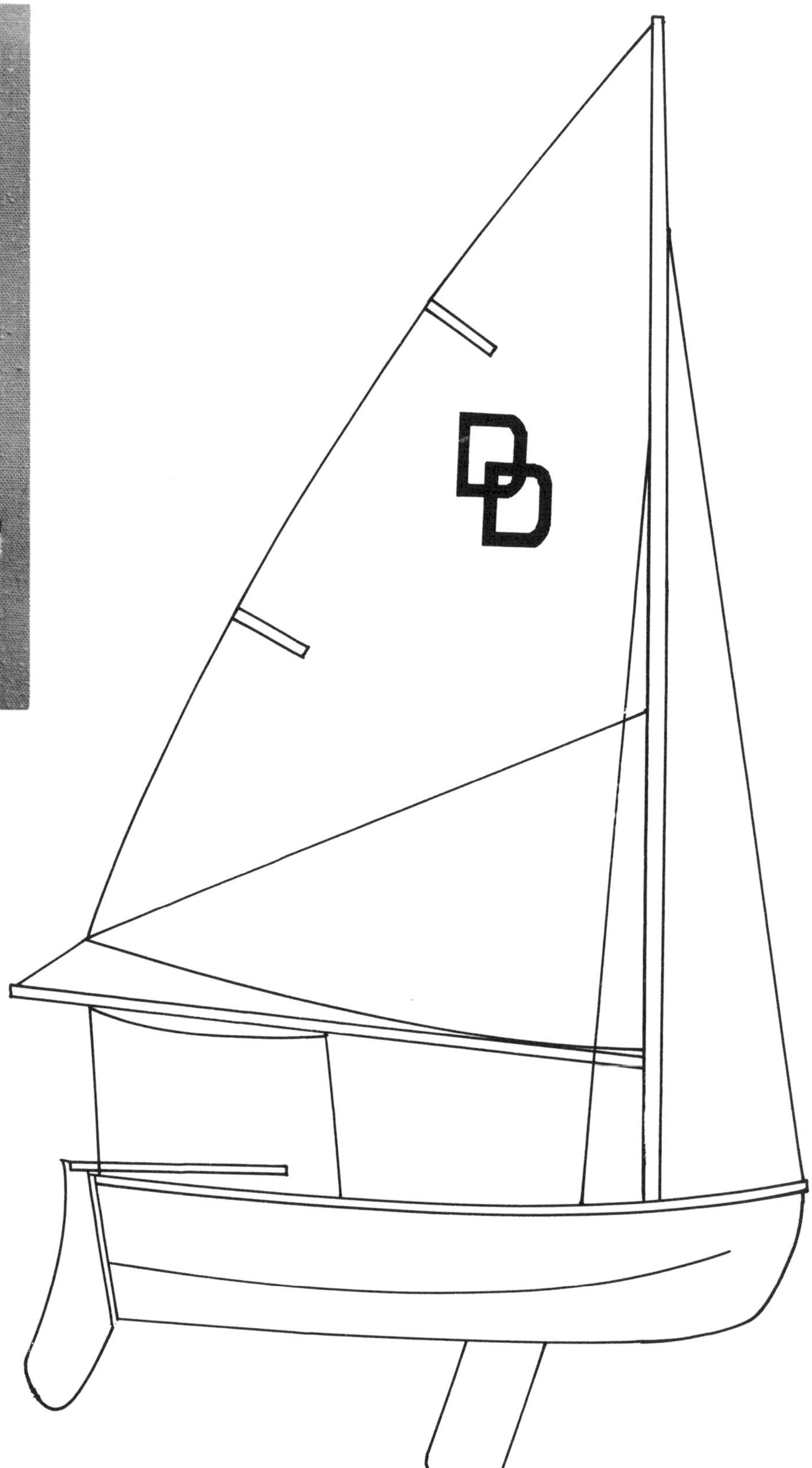

Dyer Dhow 9-foot

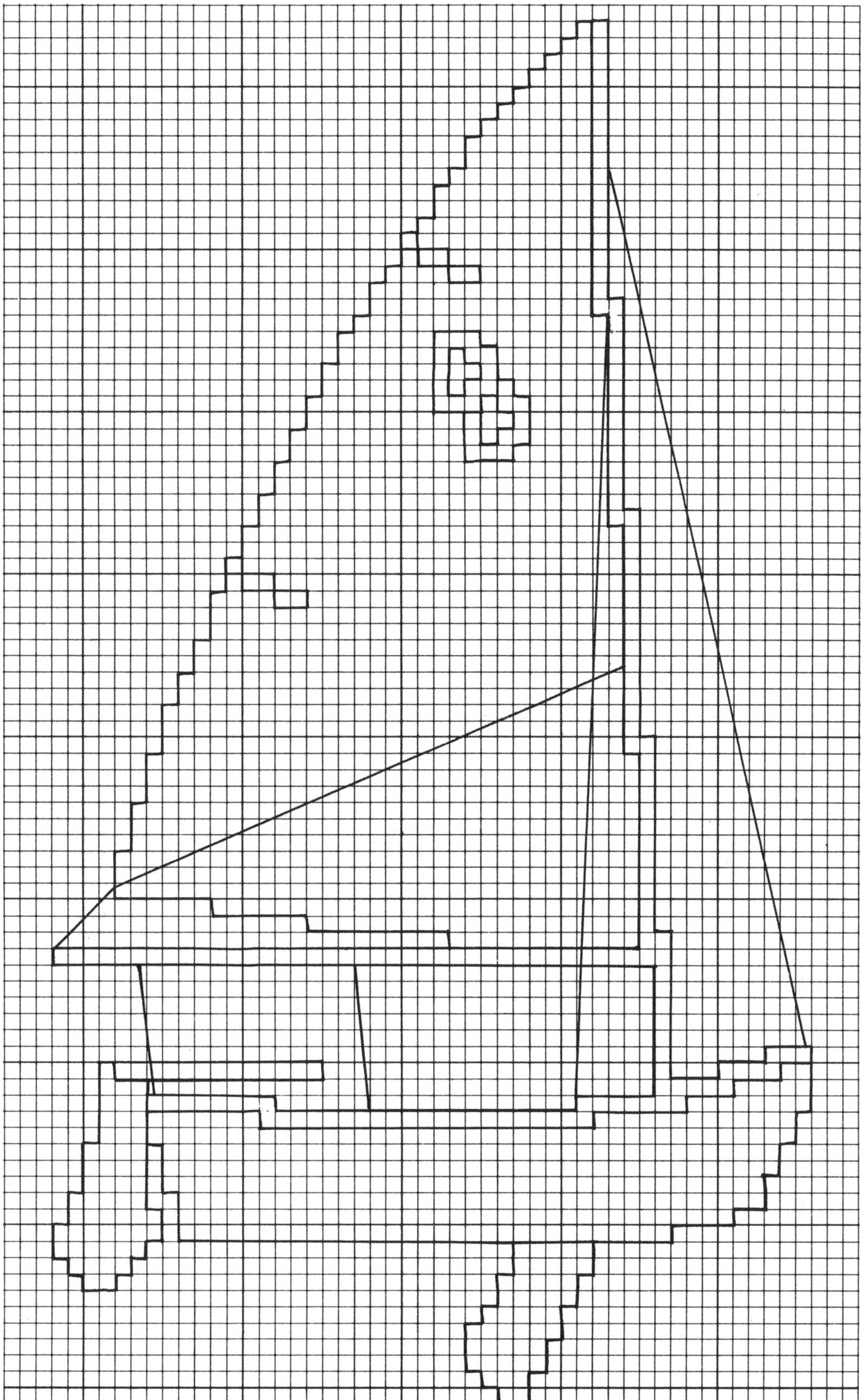

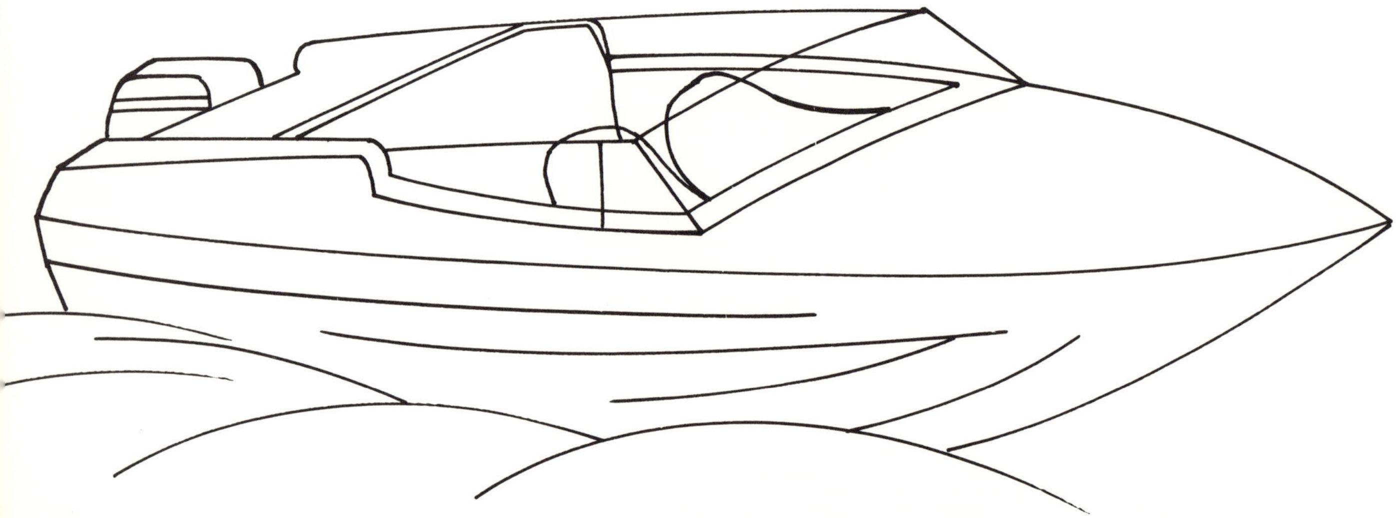

Runabouts and Speedboats

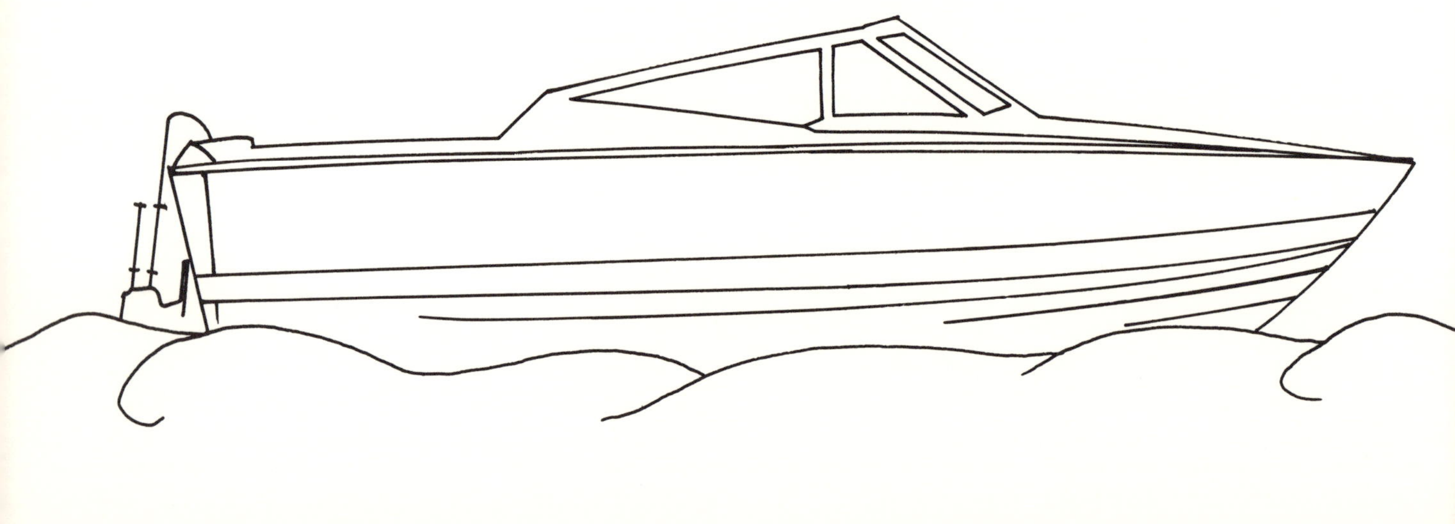

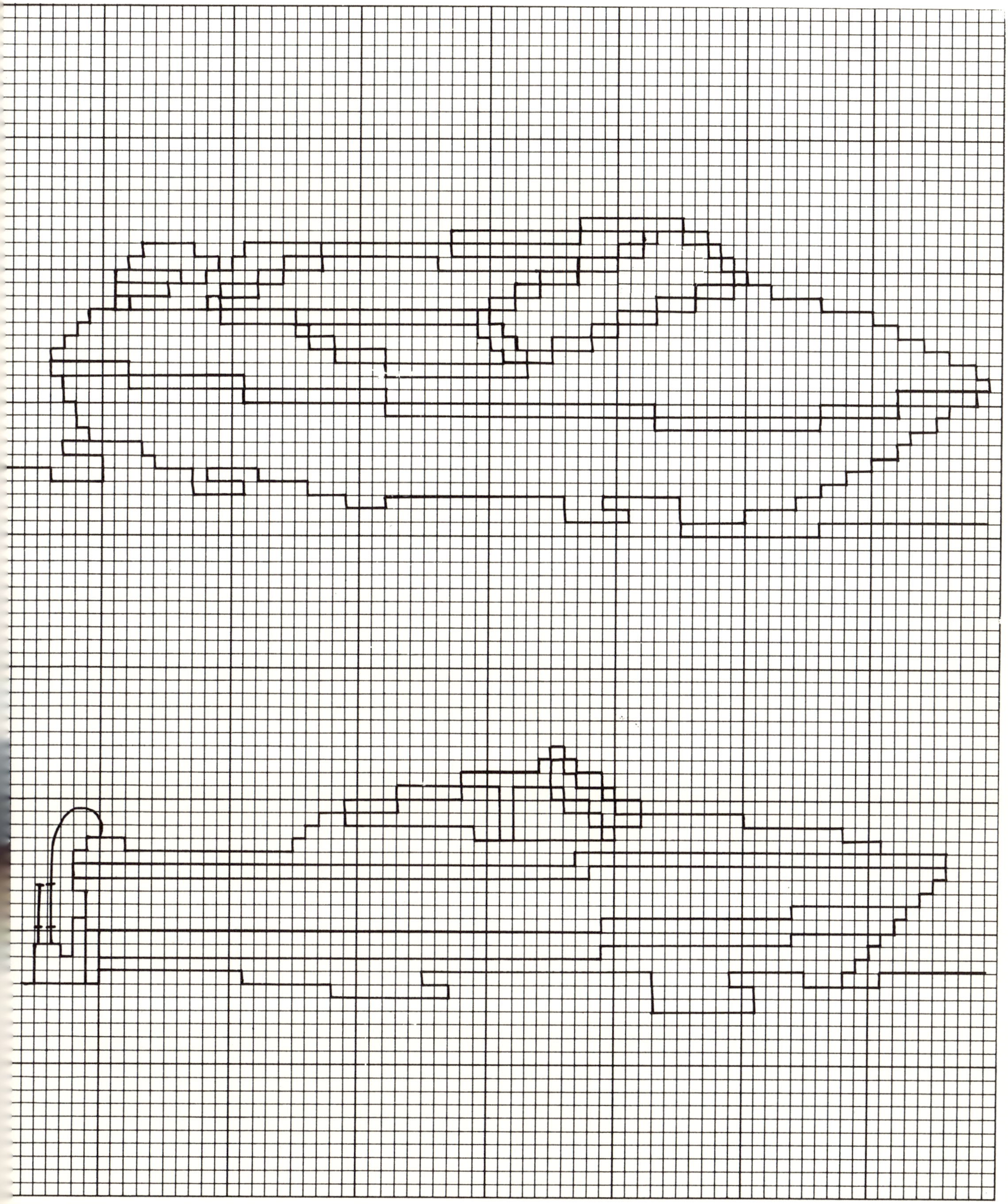

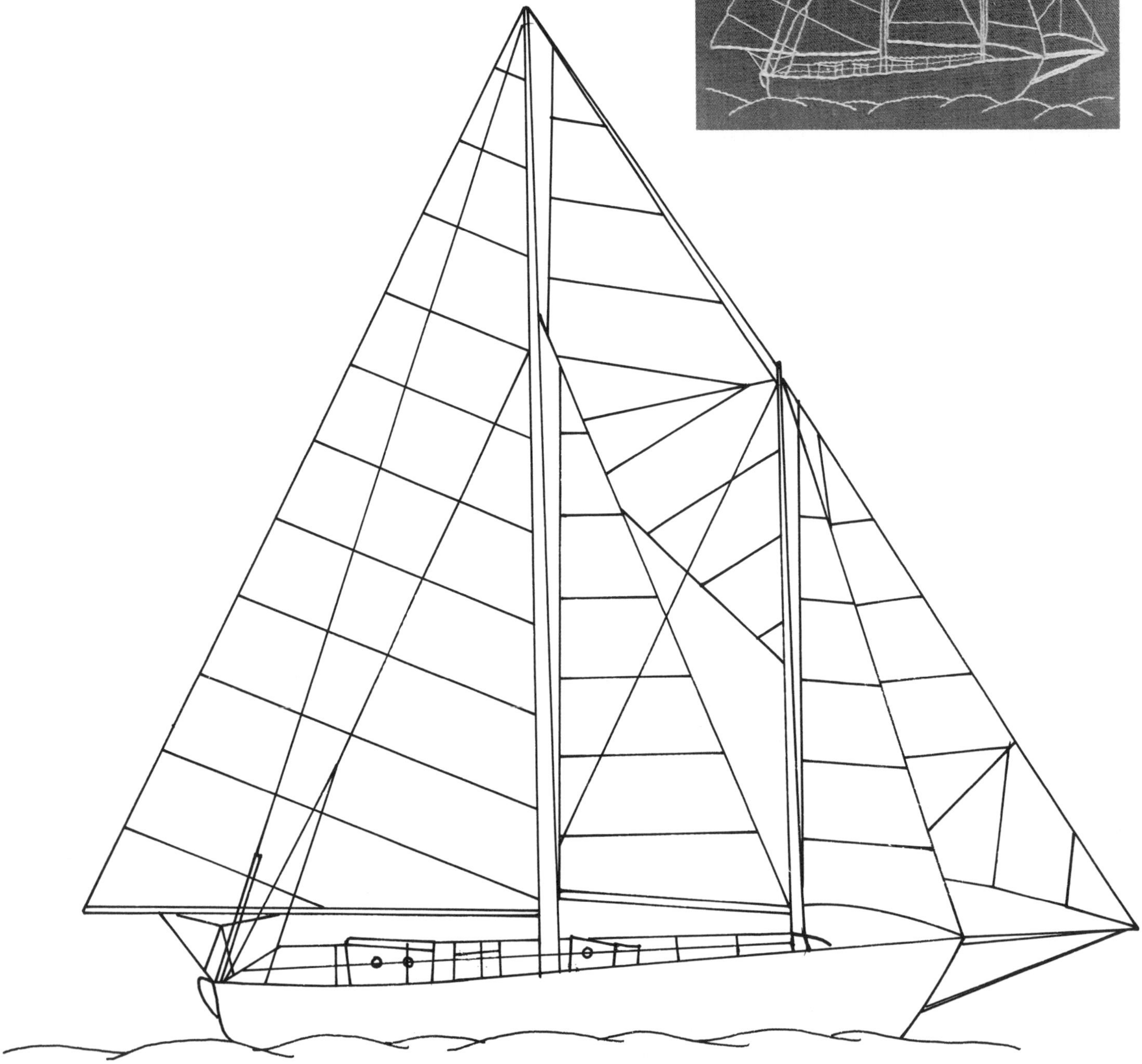

Nina, Racing Schooner

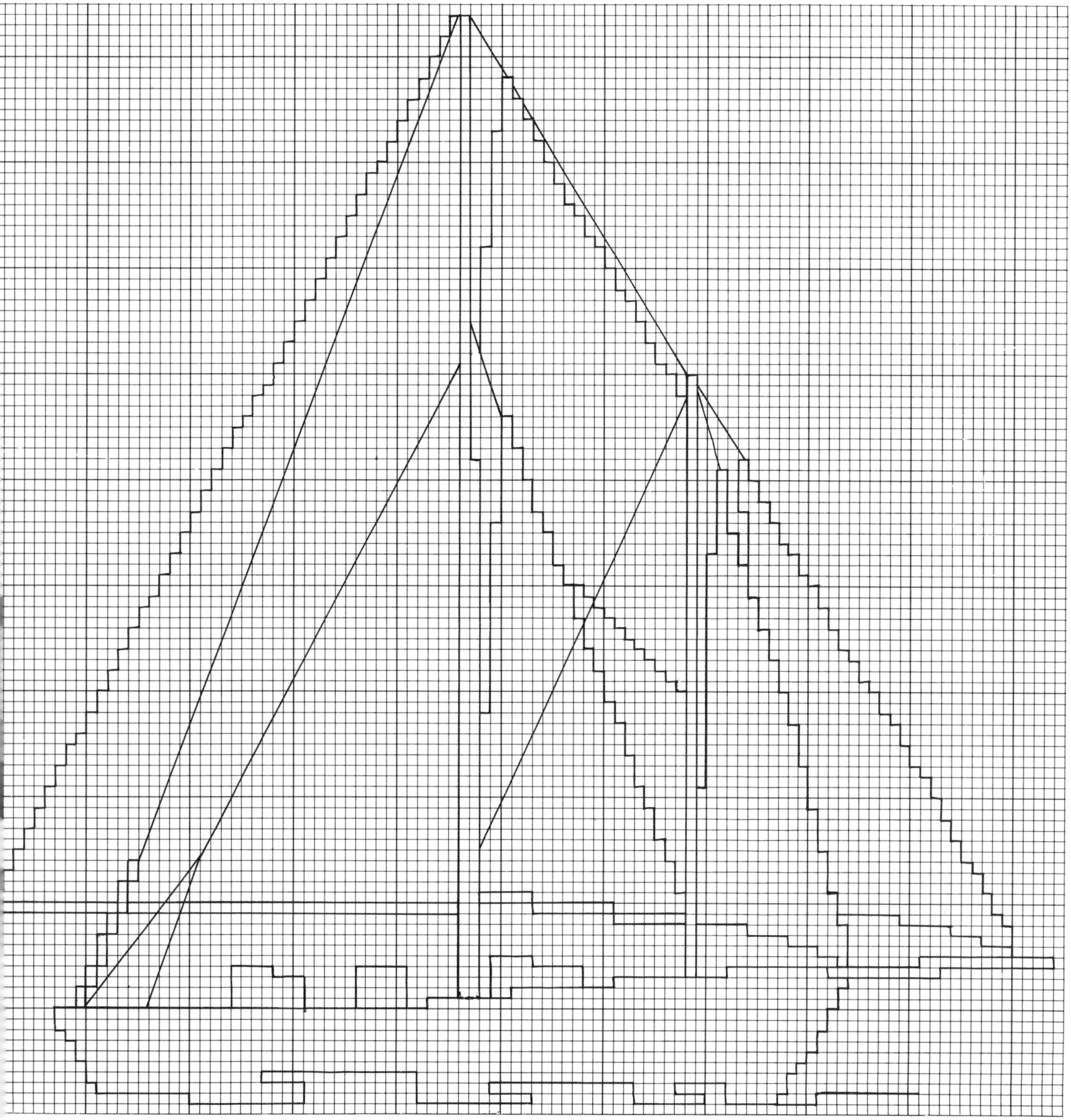

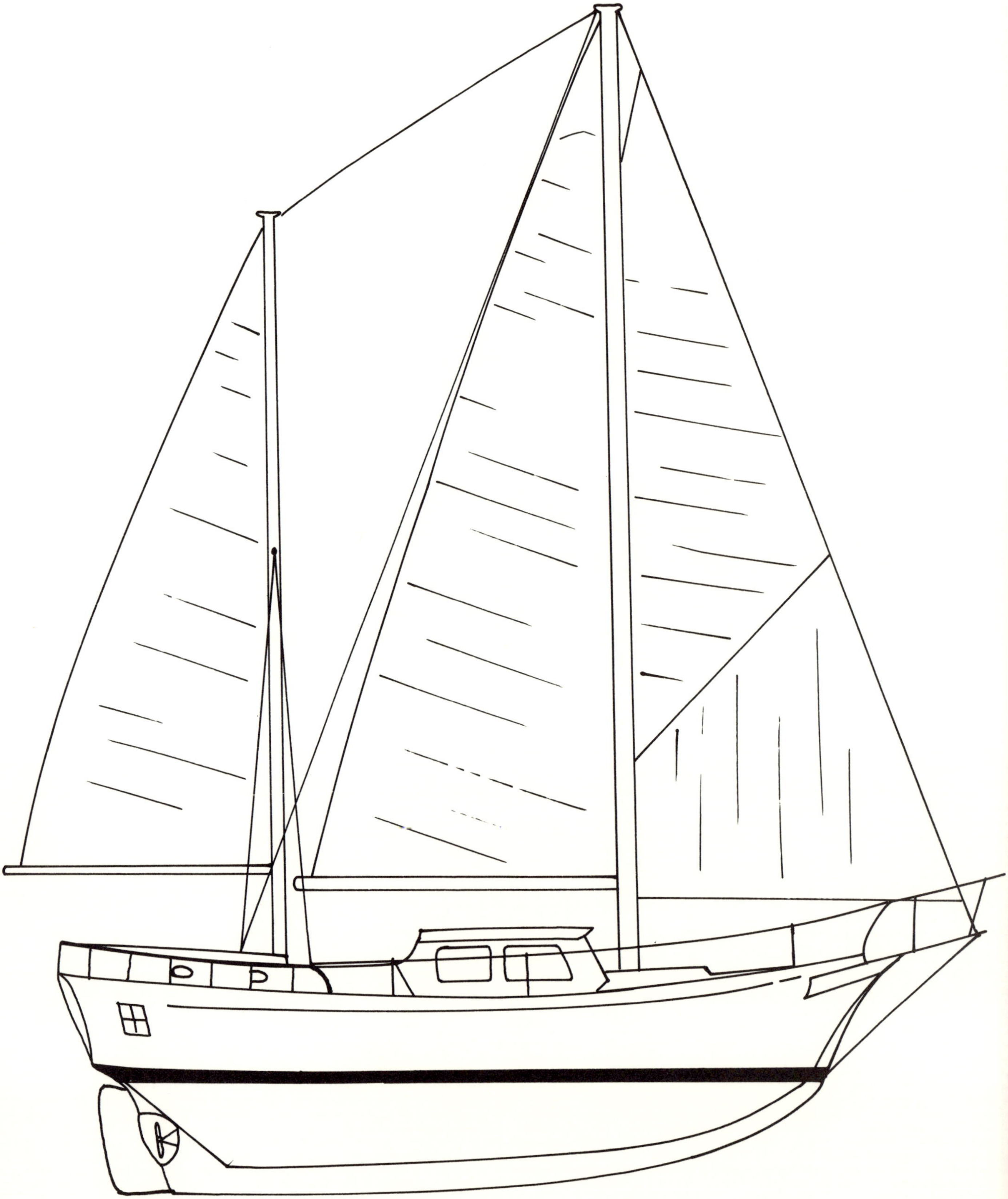

Islander 40, Motor Sailer *See Title Page*

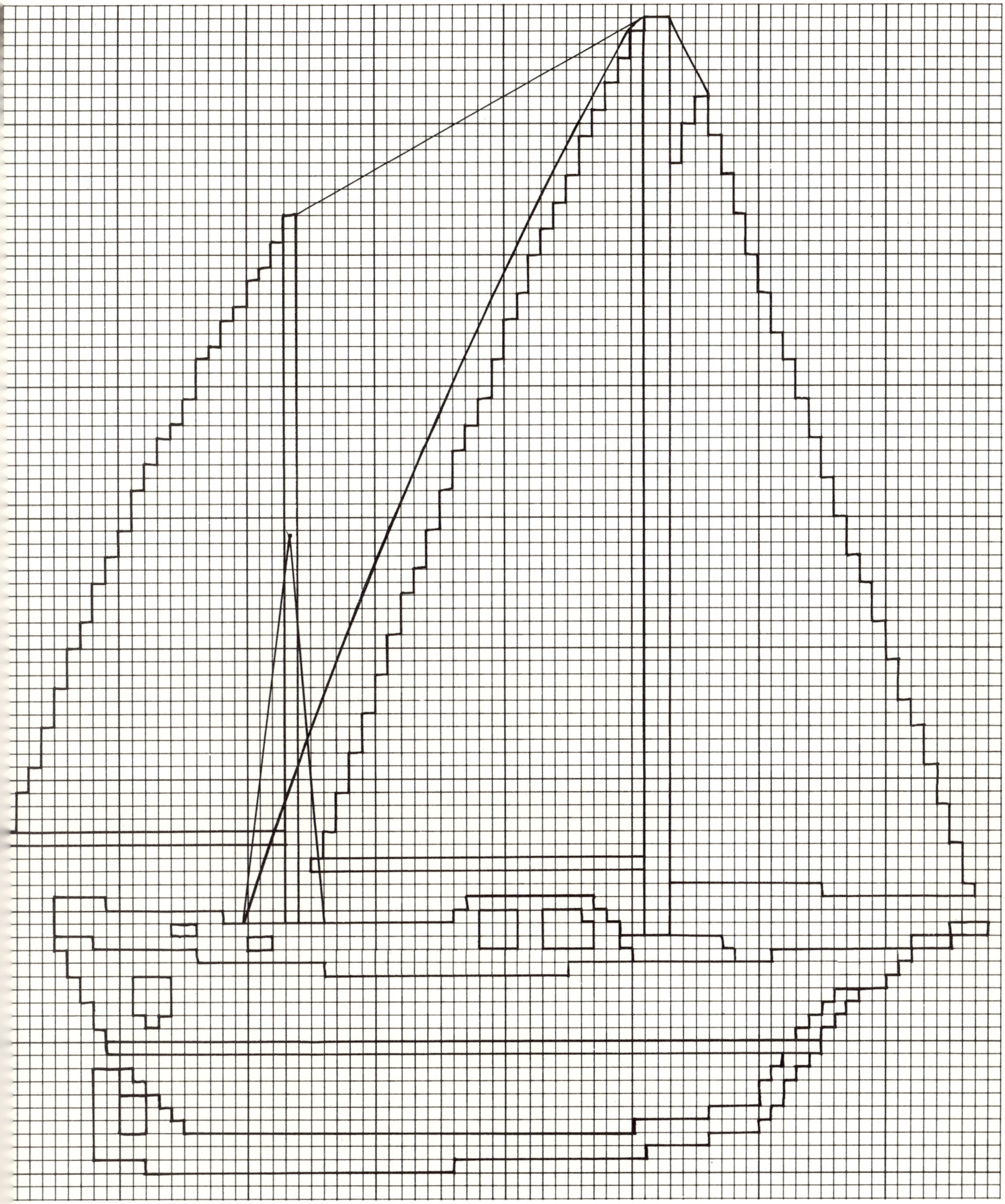

Drake's Galleon, from Op Sail *See Plate 6*

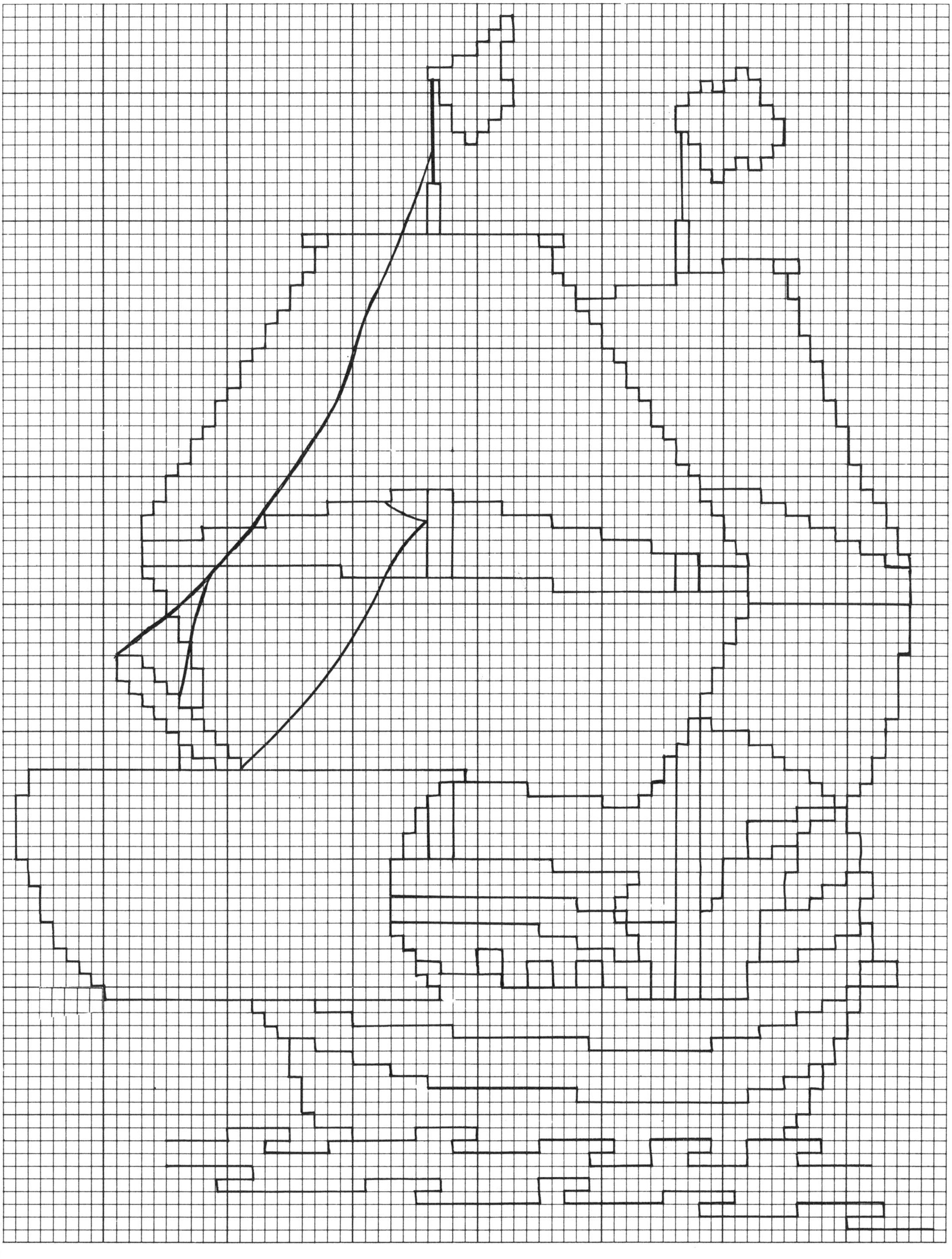

Hobie Cat *See Plate 6*

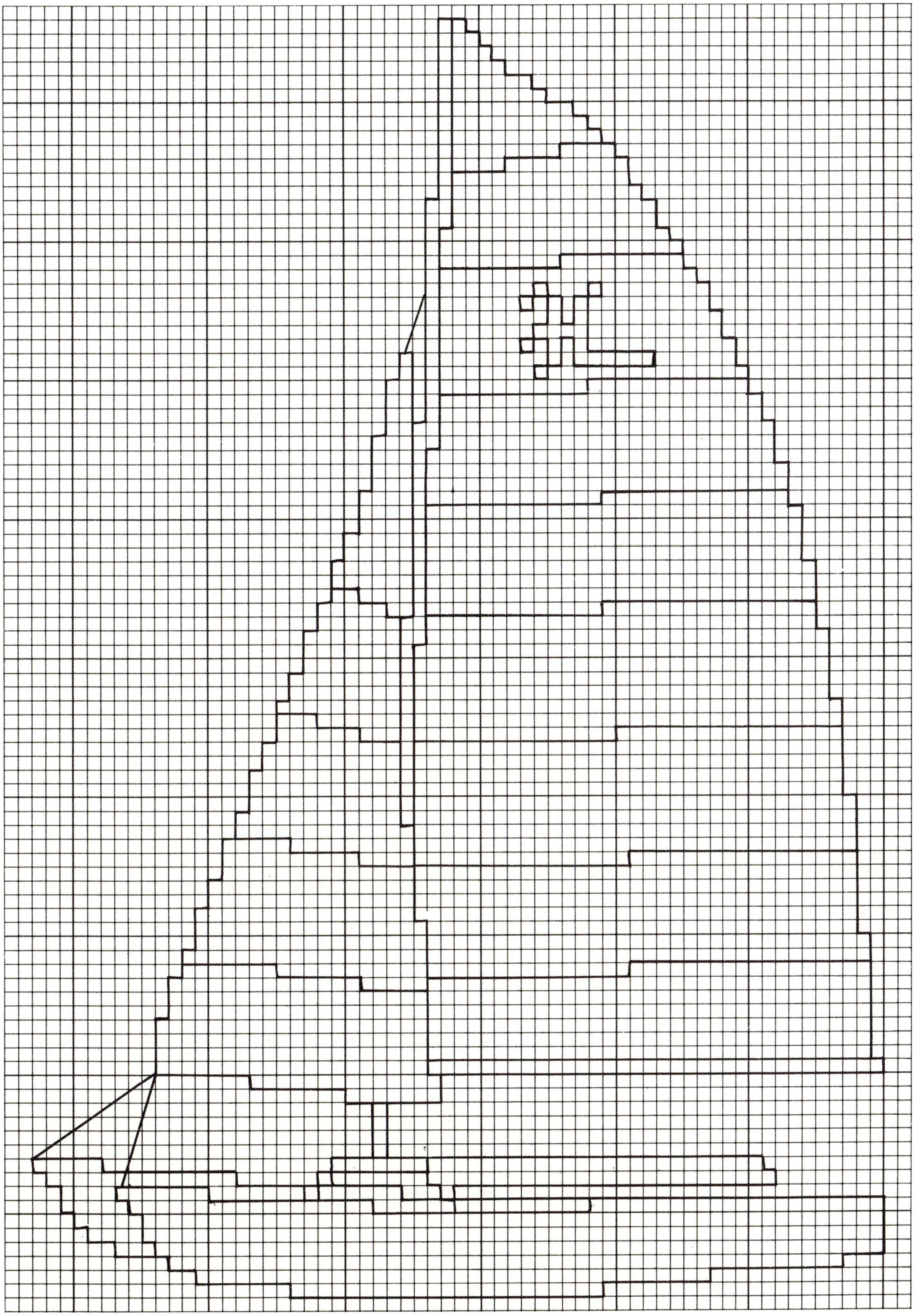

12-Meter

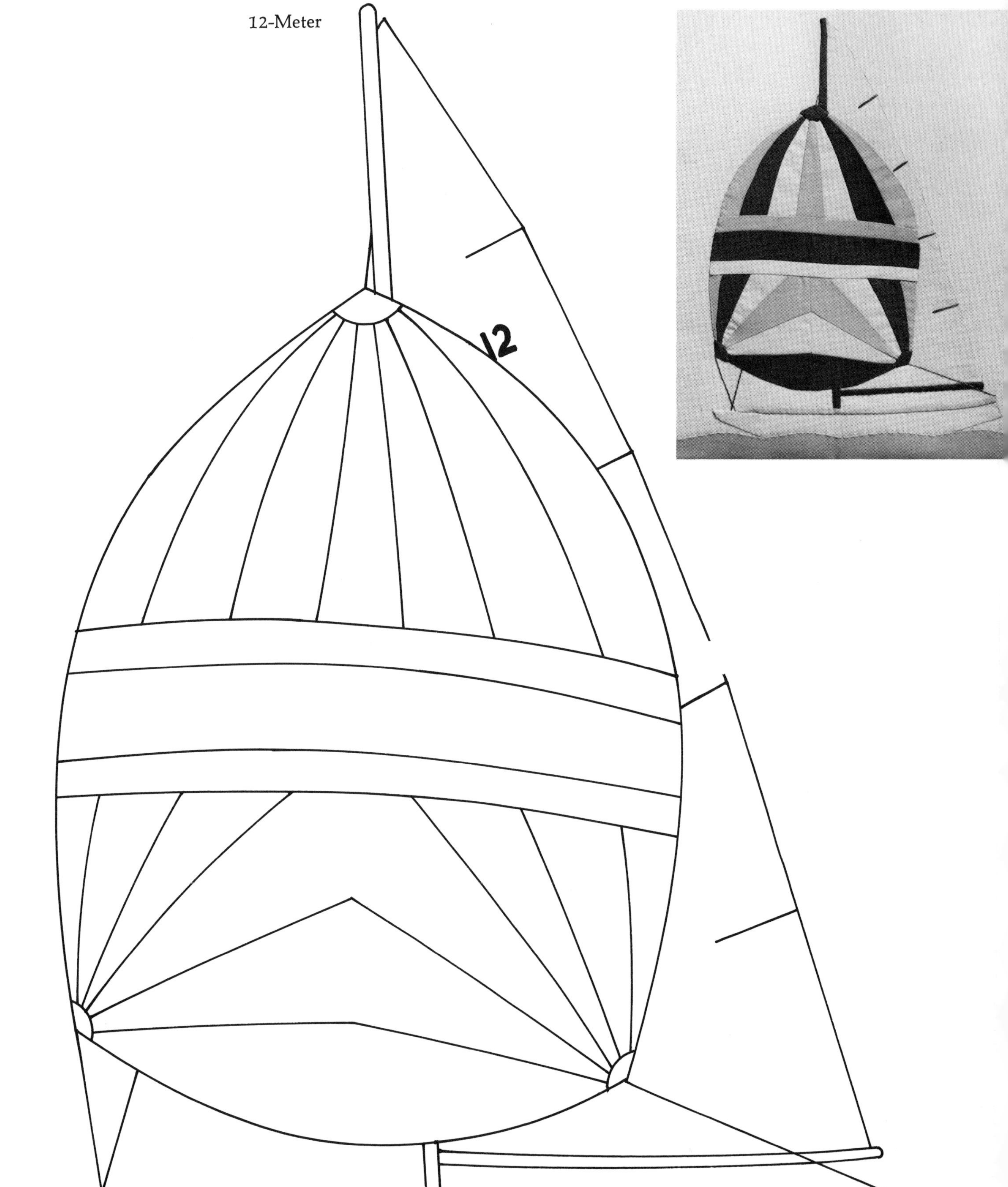

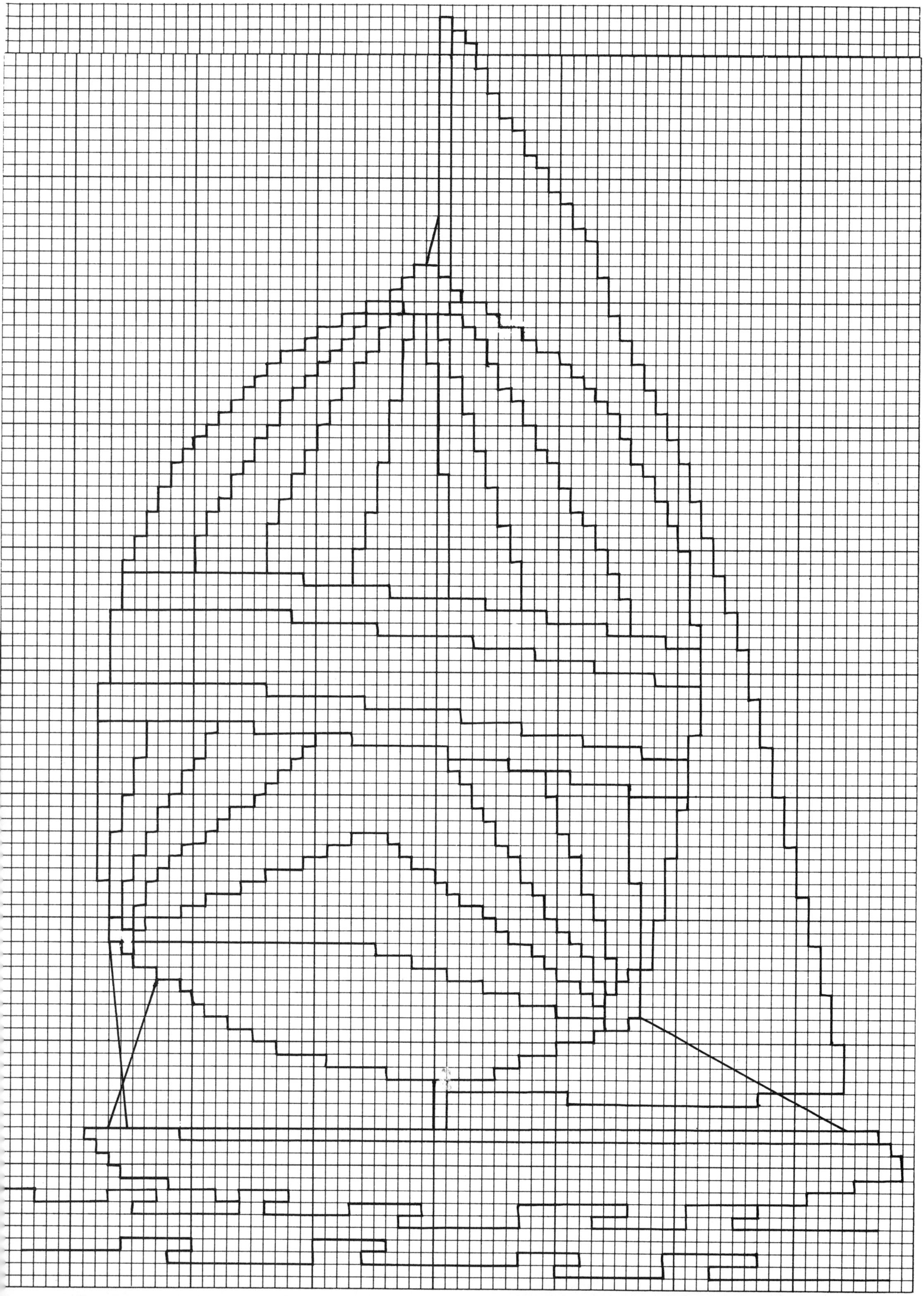

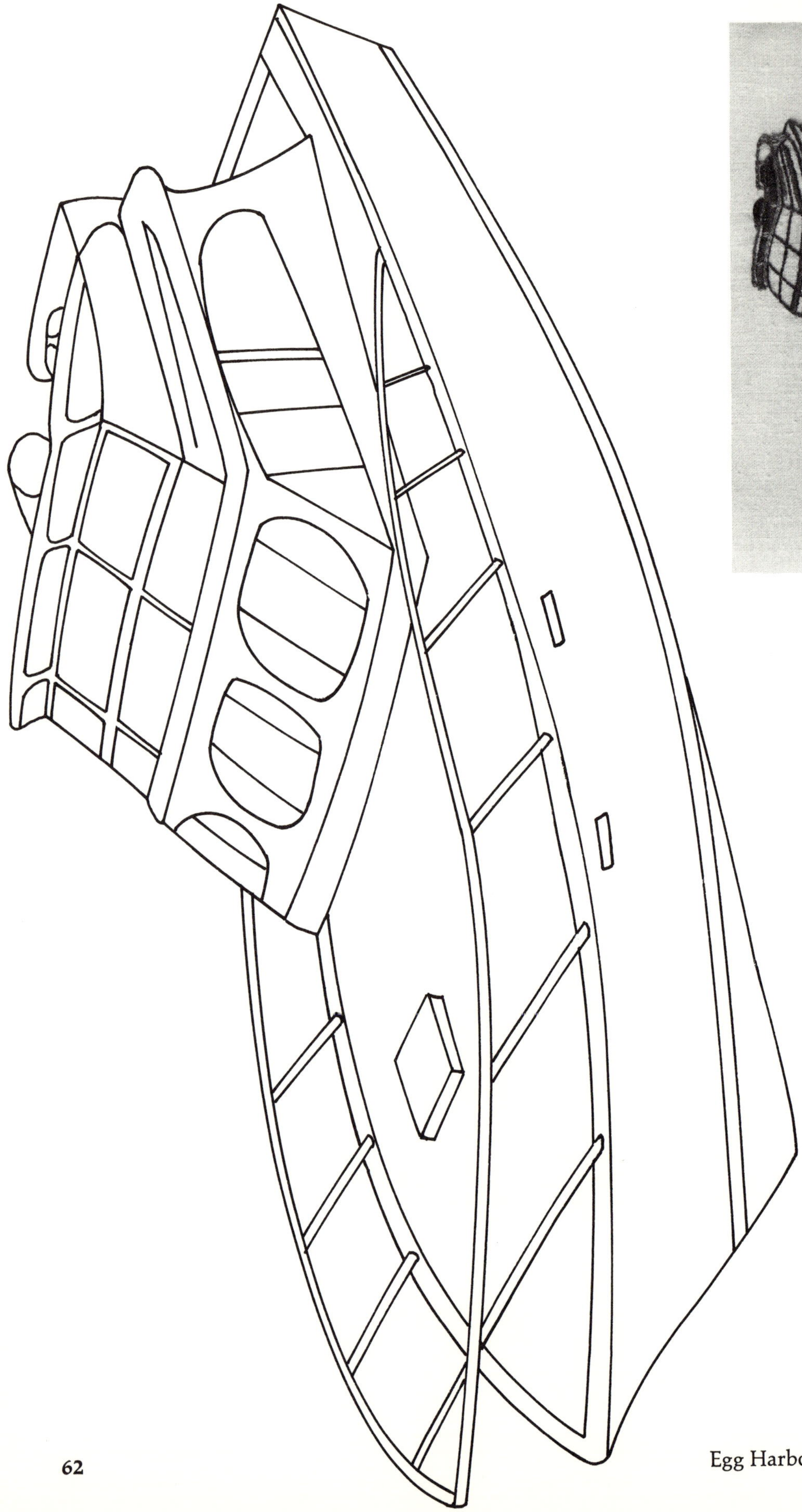

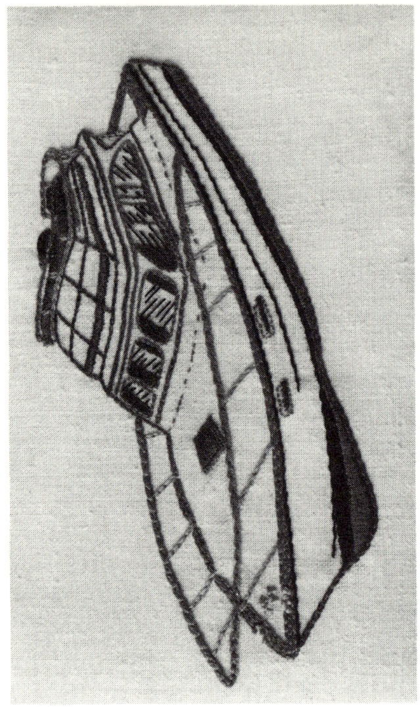

Egg Harbor 36

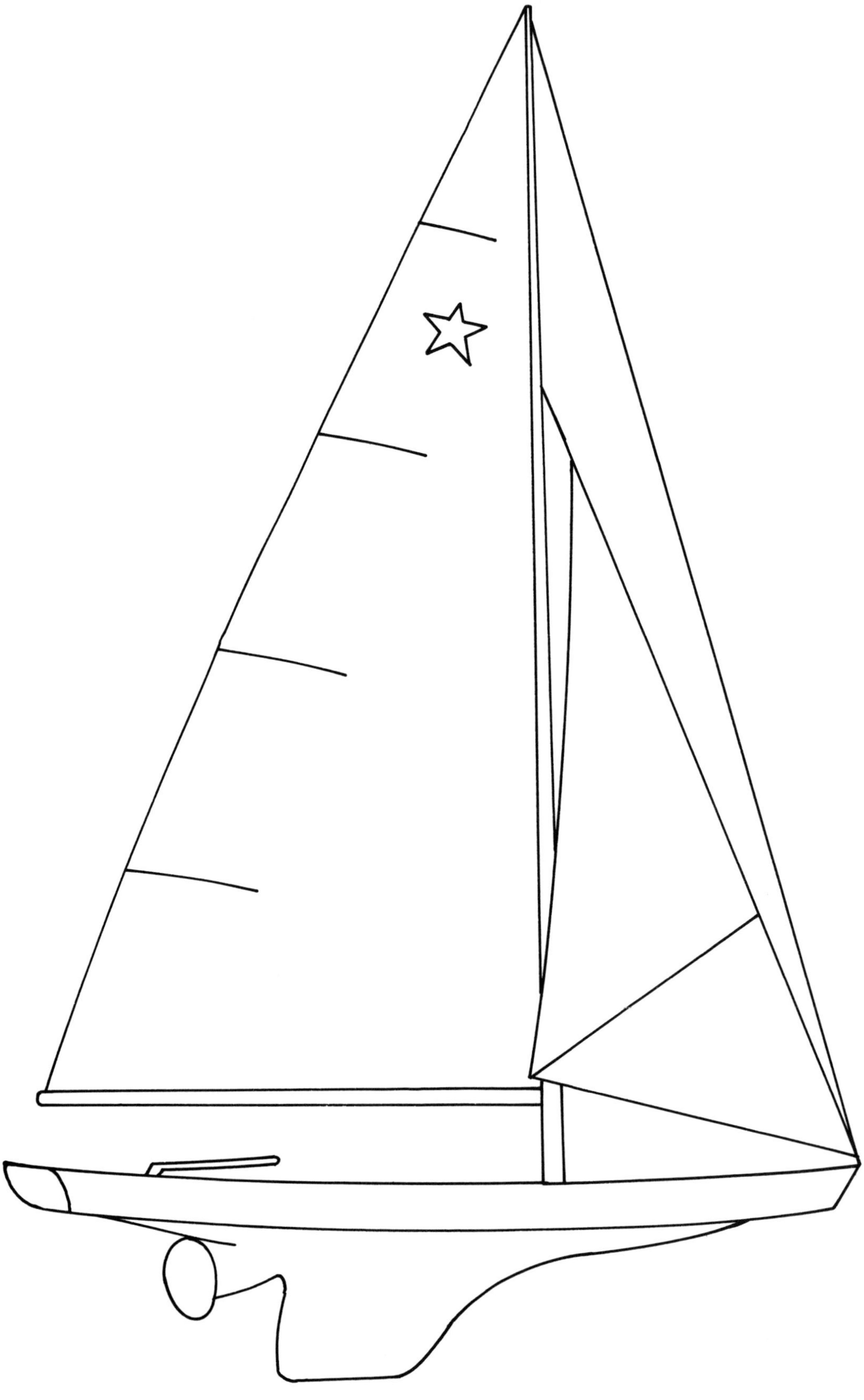

Star *See Plate 5*

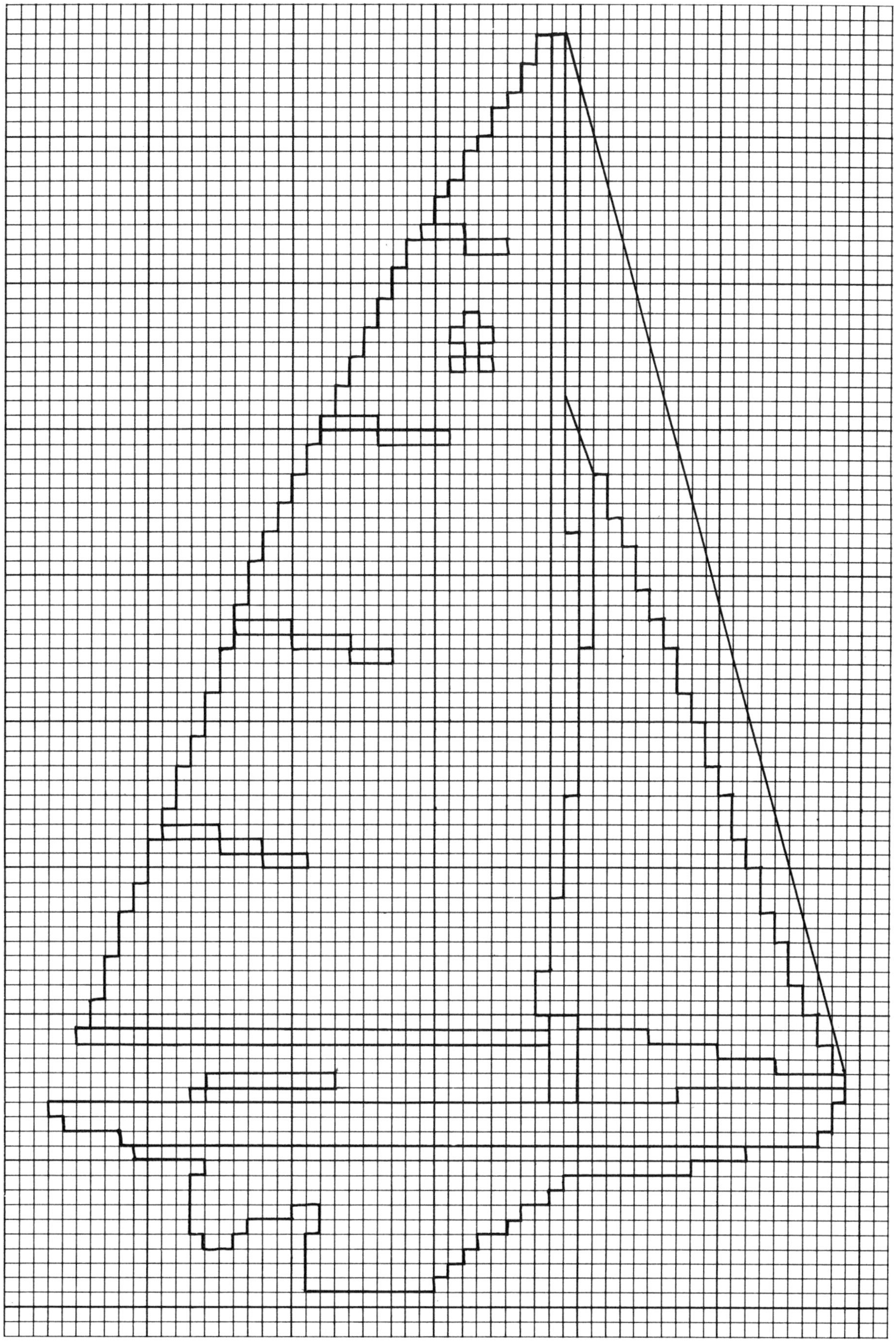

INSIGNIA

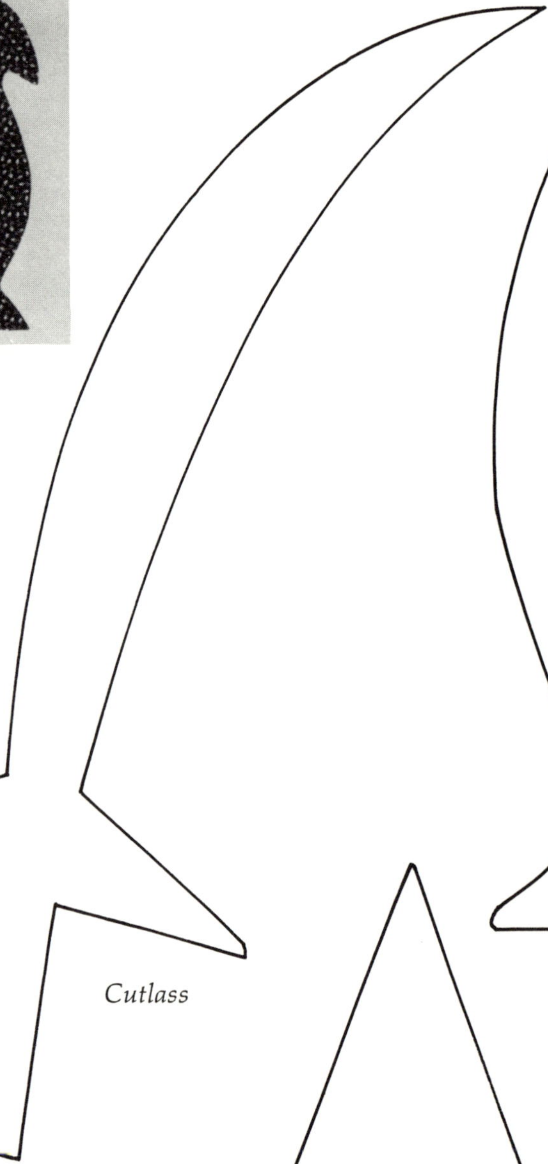

Cutlass

Penguin

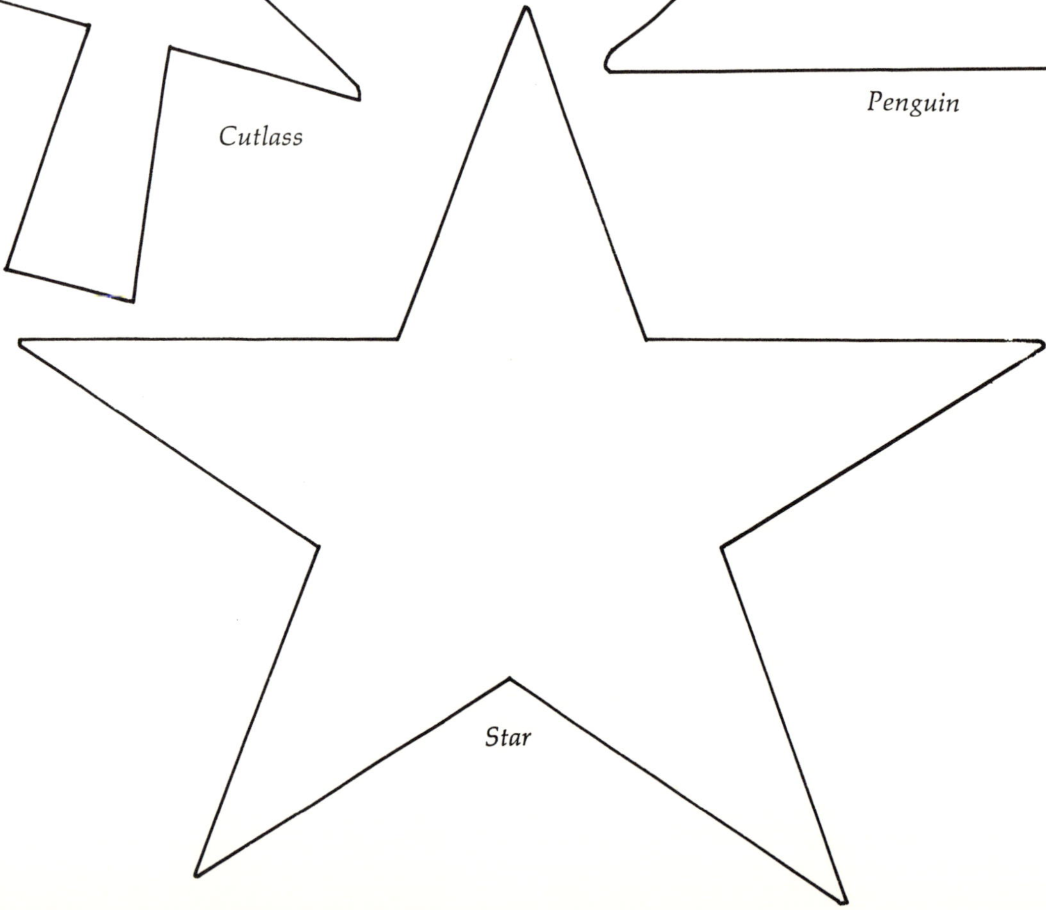

Star

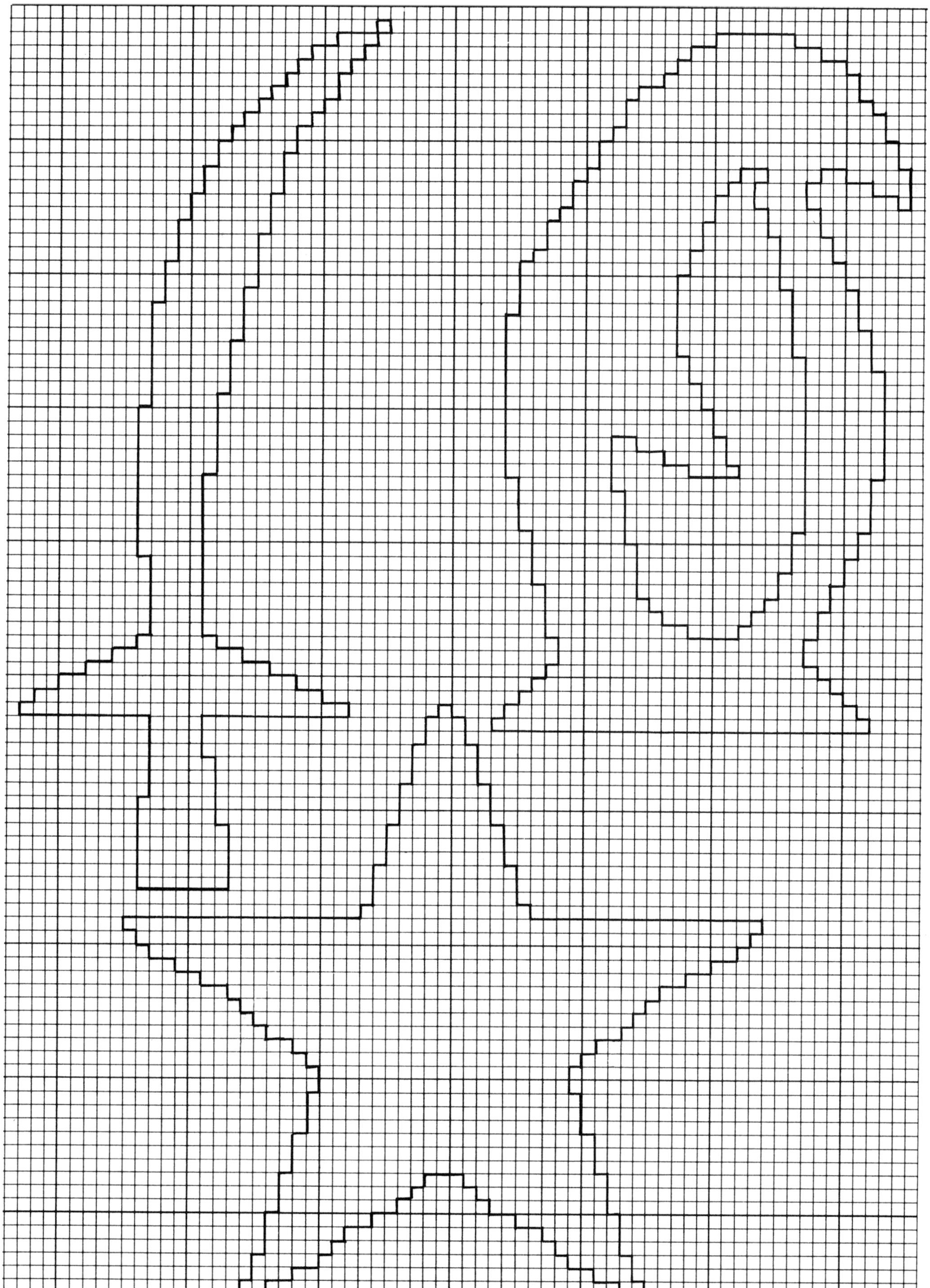

See Plate 8

Sunfish

See Plate 8

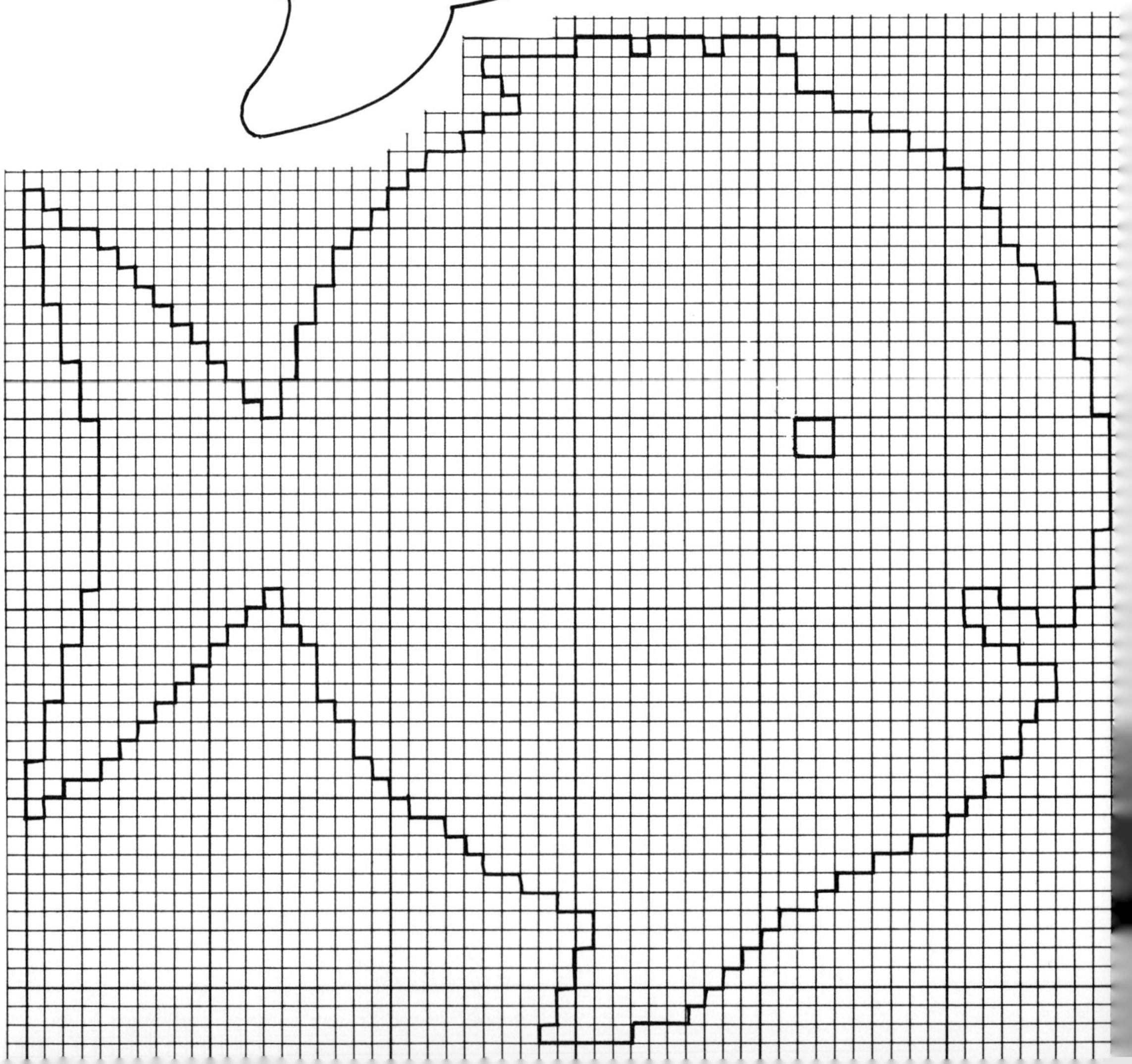

Chesapeake 20

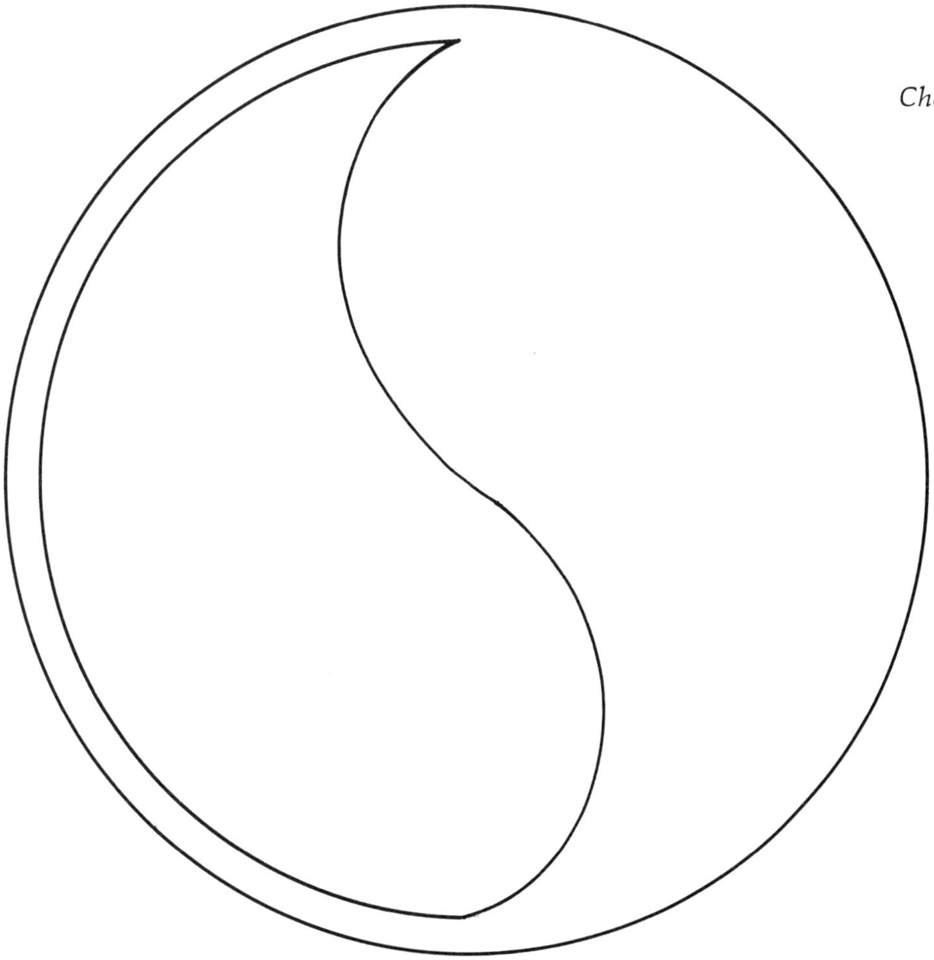

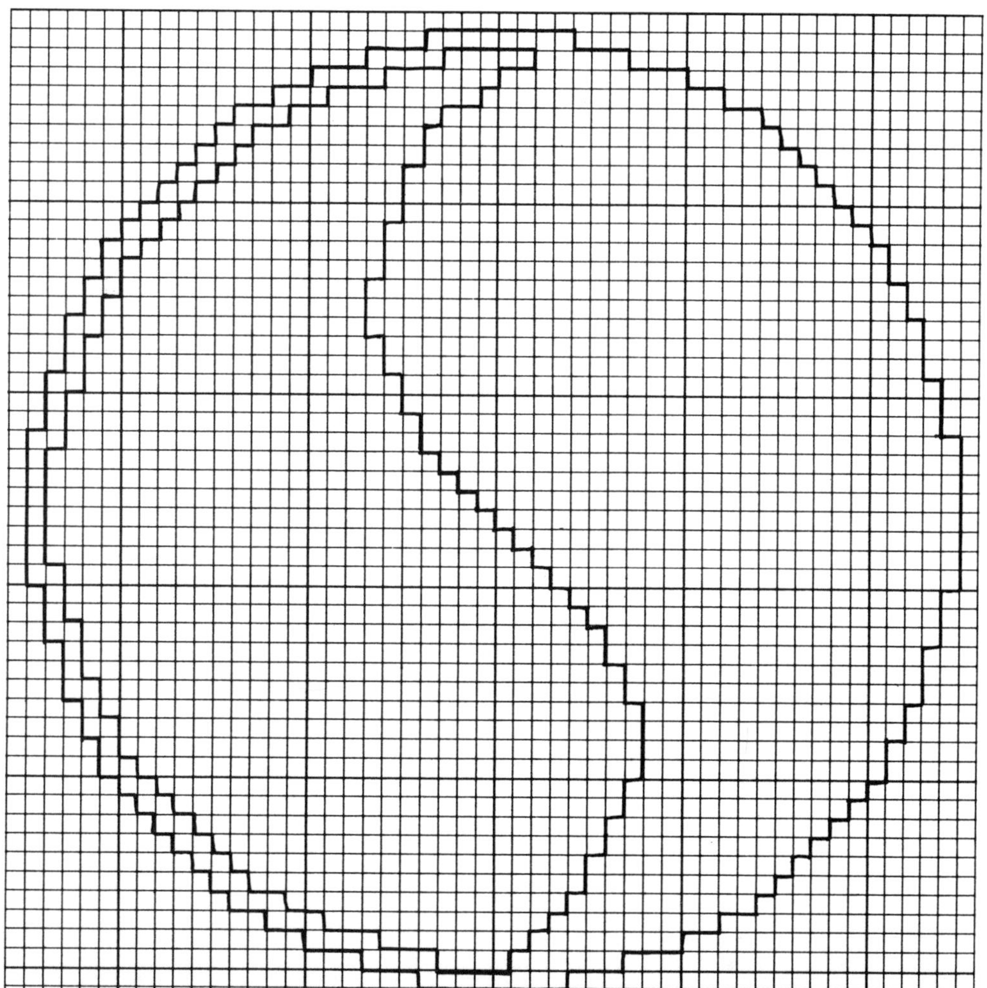

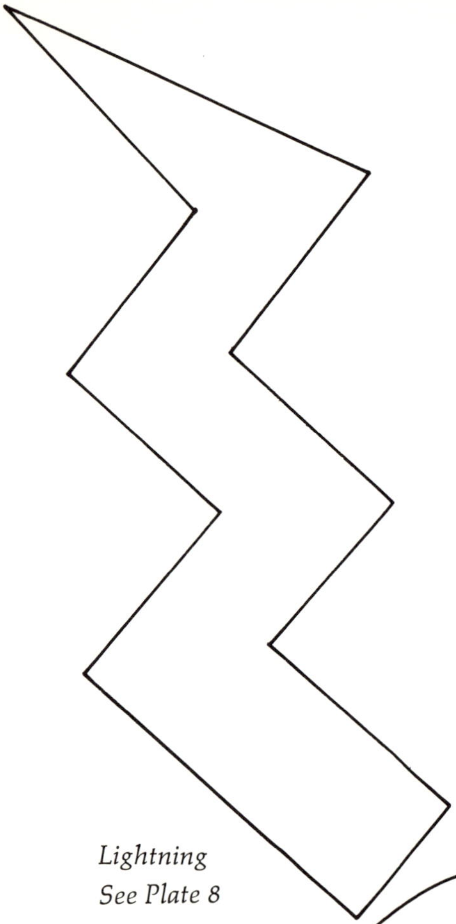

Lightning
See Plate 8

Columbia 29

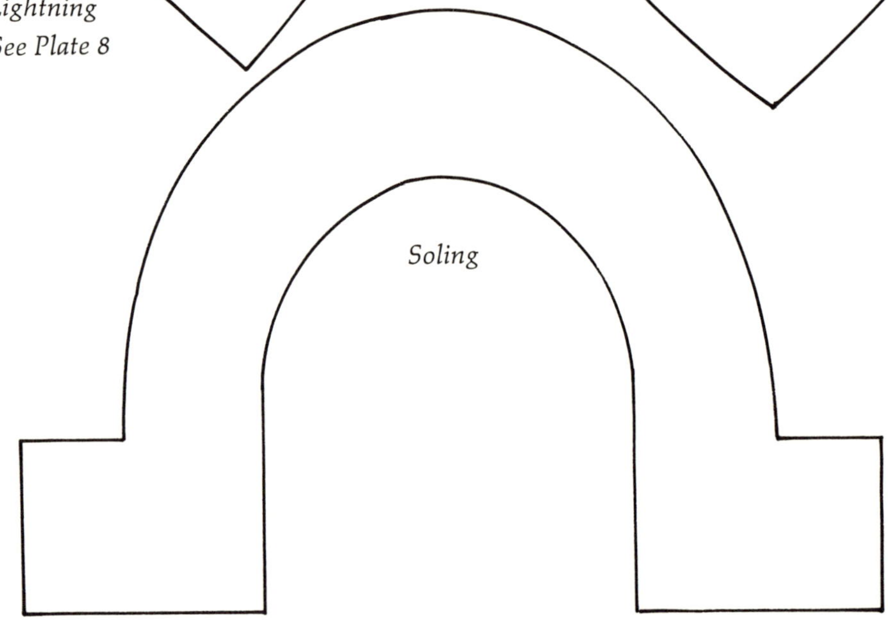

Soling

Tiki II

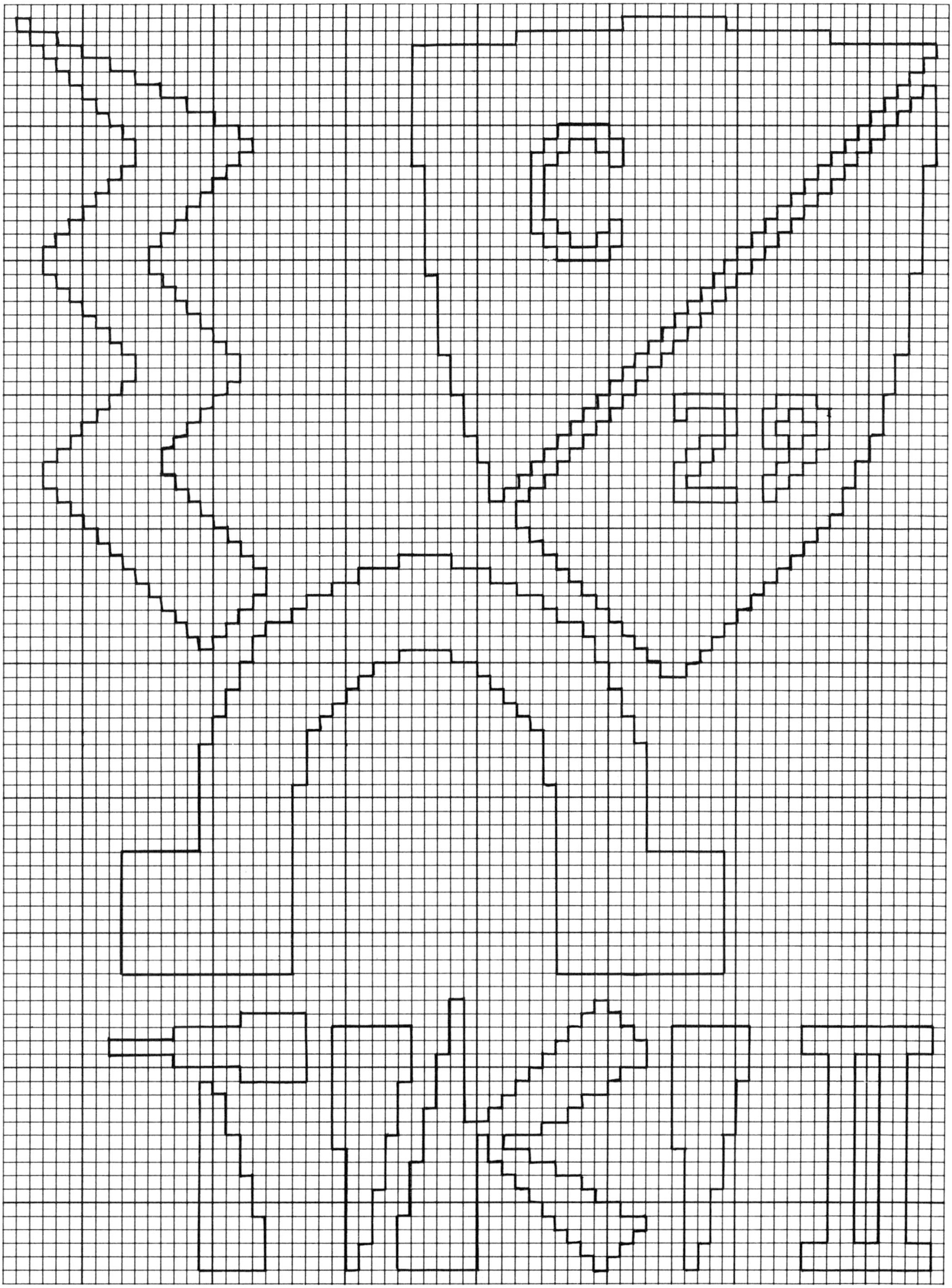

See Plate 8

U.S. Power Squadron's Ensign *See Plate 3*

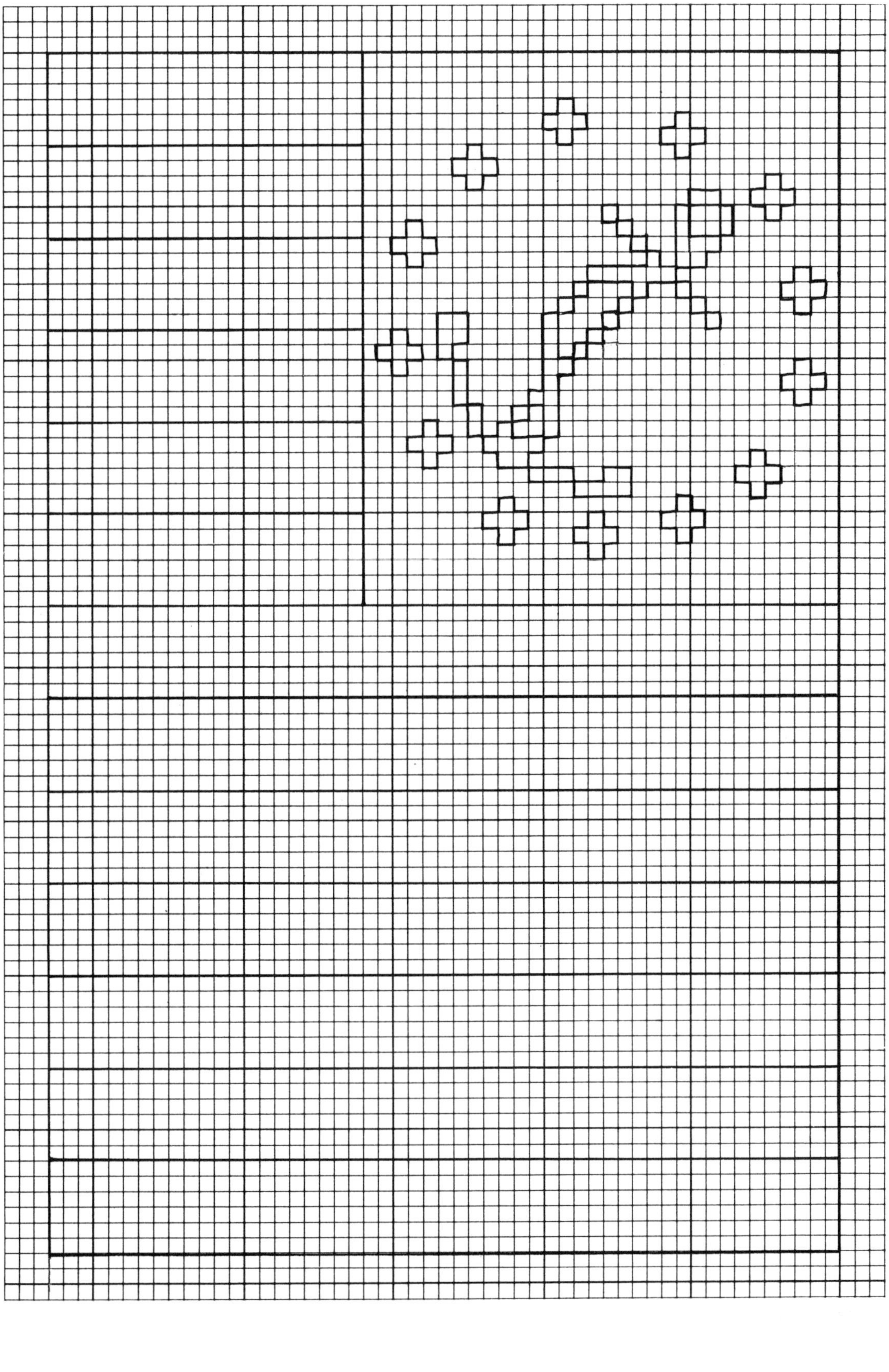

U.S. Yacht Racing Union

See Plate 2

Compass Rose *See Plate 5*

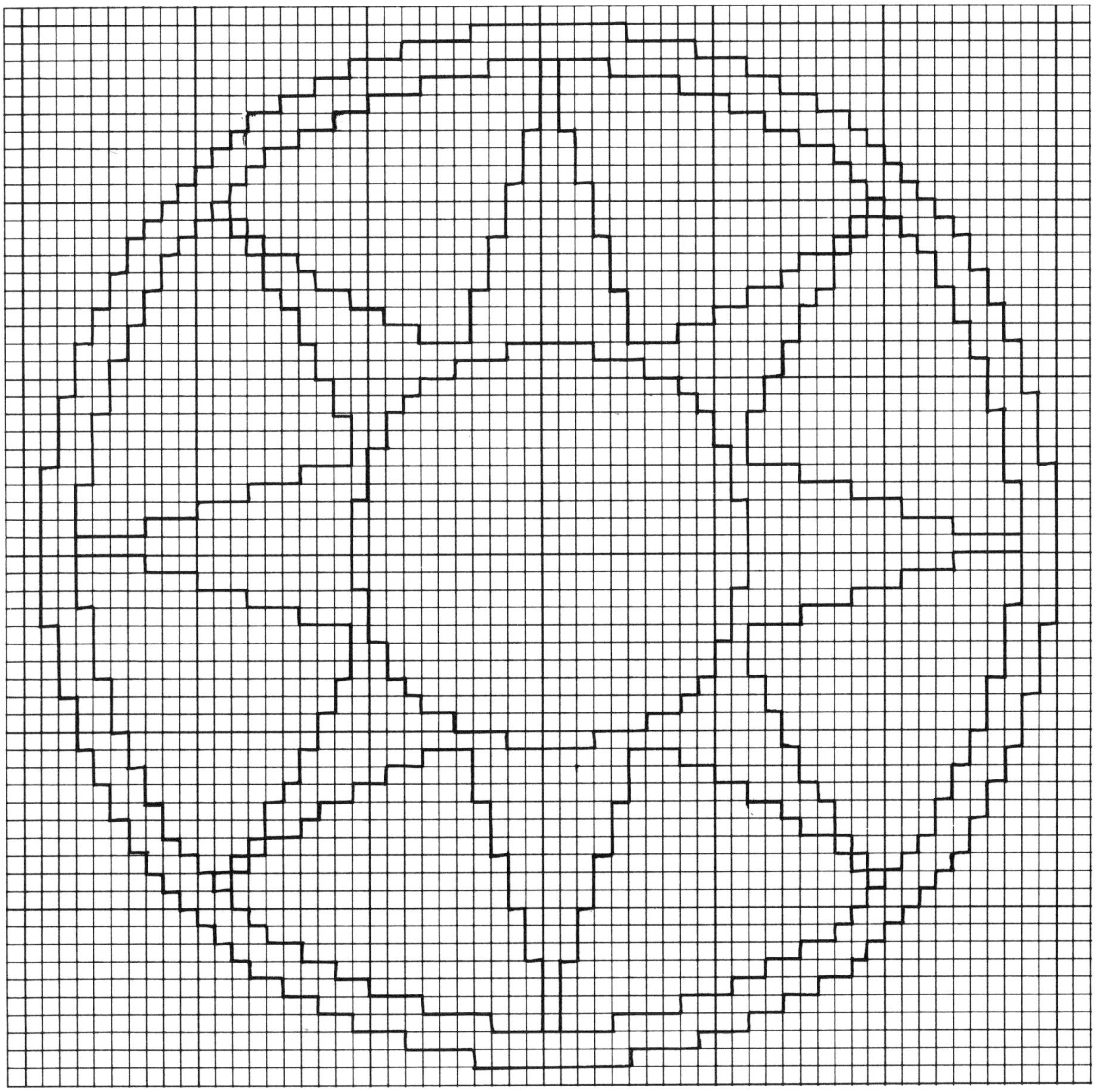

BUOYS AND LIGHTHOUSE

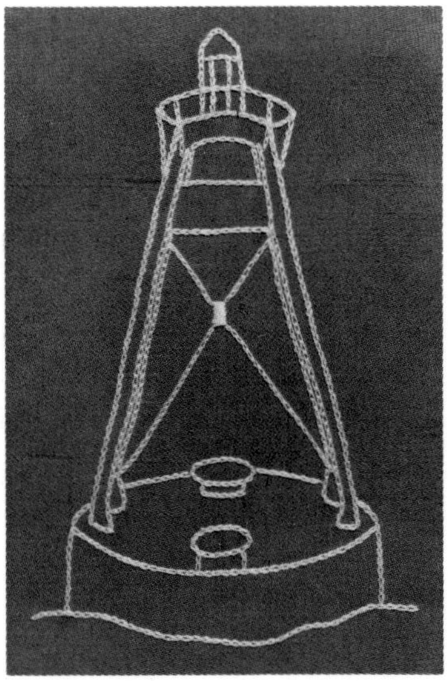

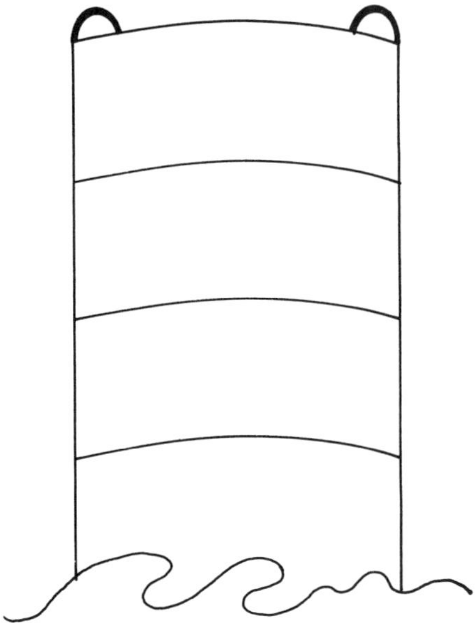

Mid-channel Can

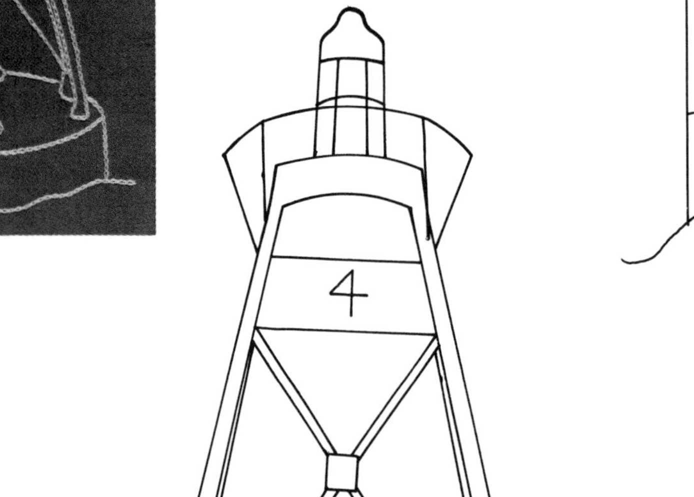

Light buoy

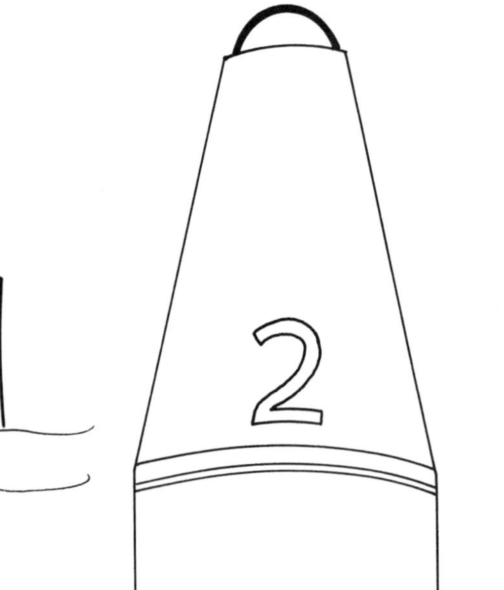

Nun

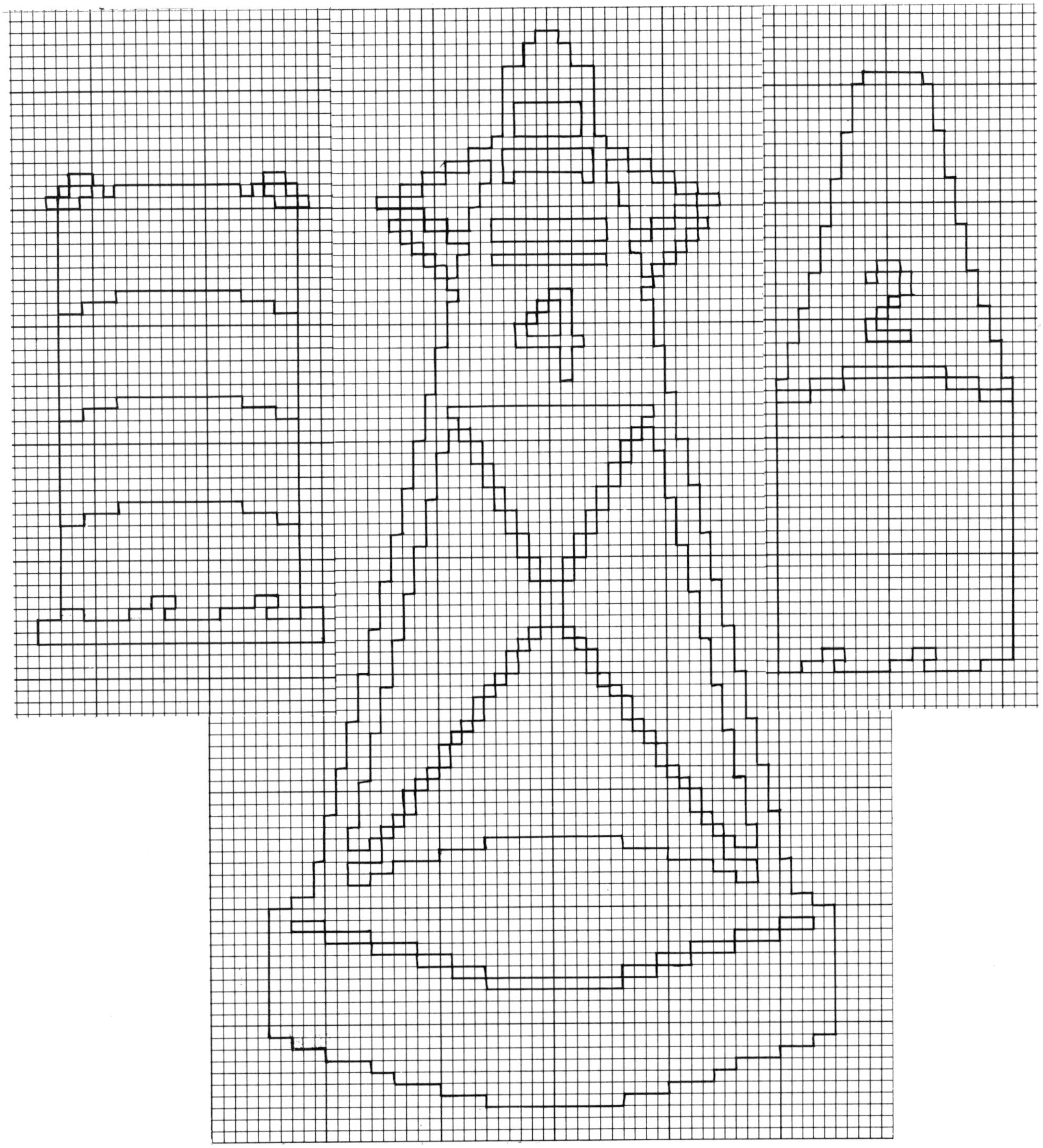

Lighthouse

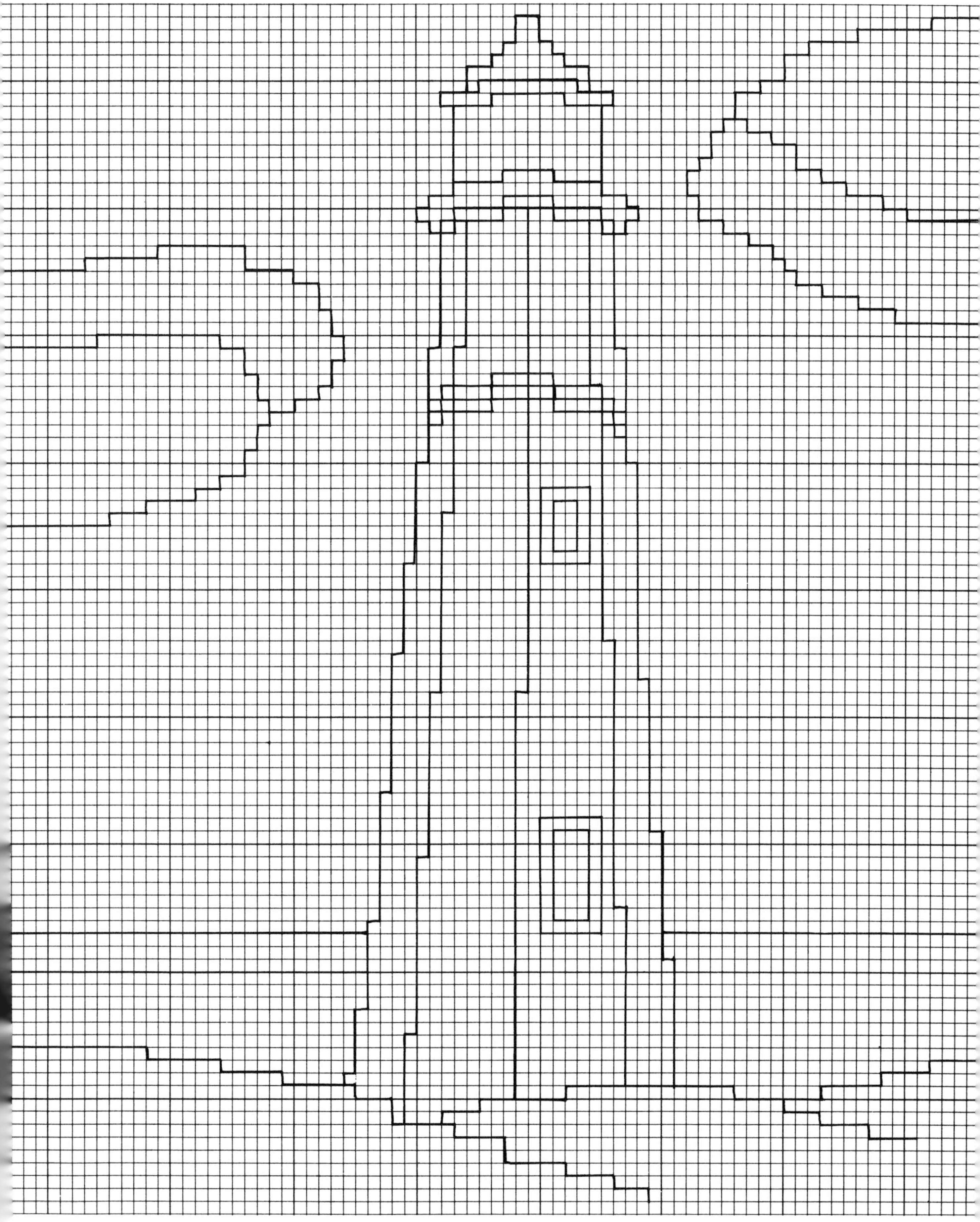

CODE FLAGS

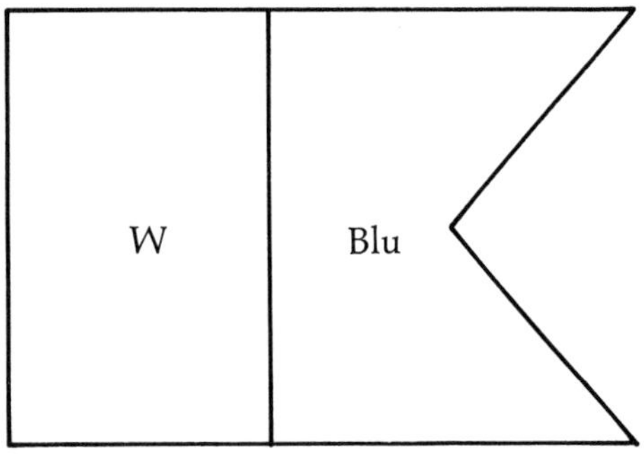

A

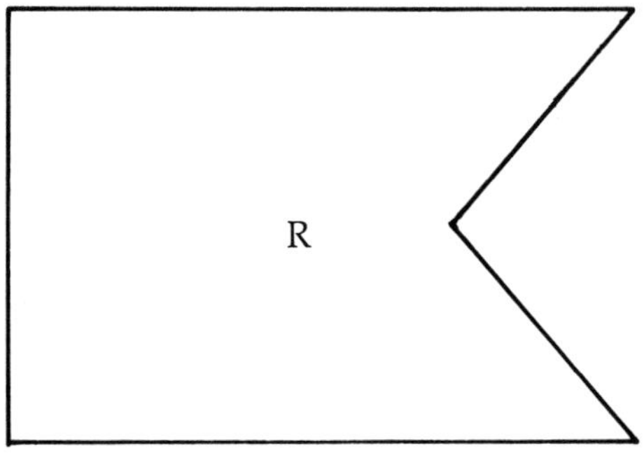

B

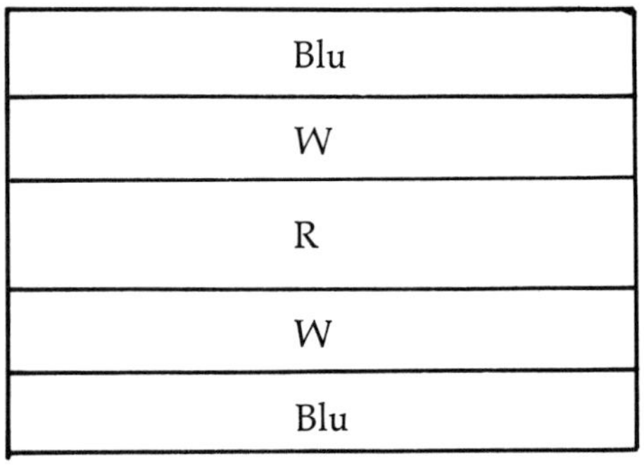

C

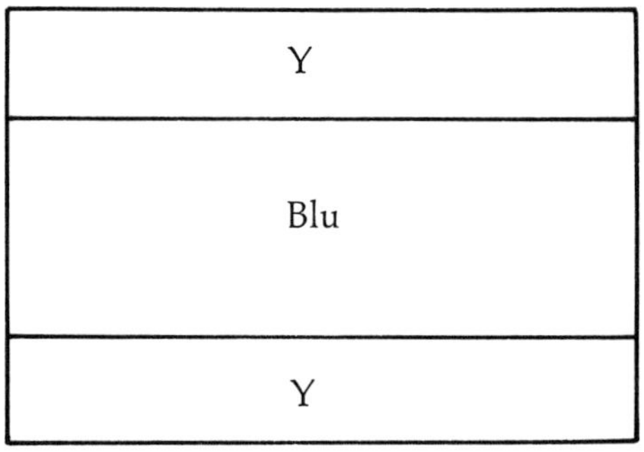

D

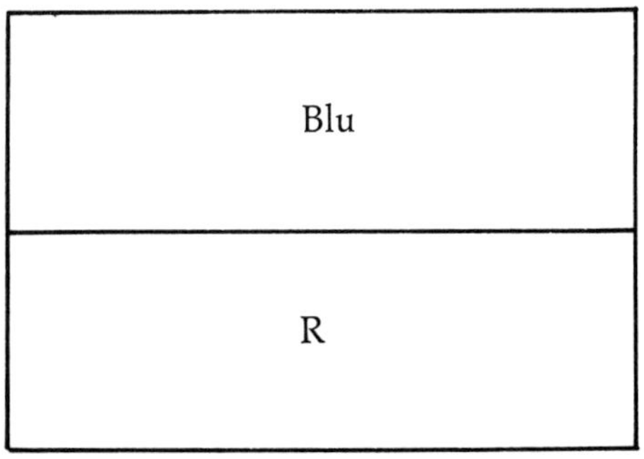

E

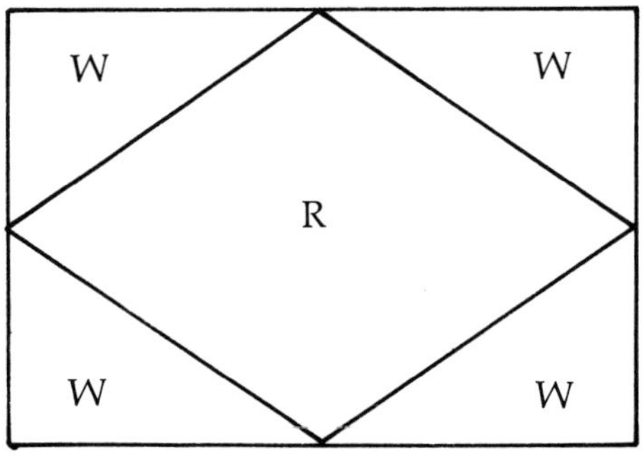

F

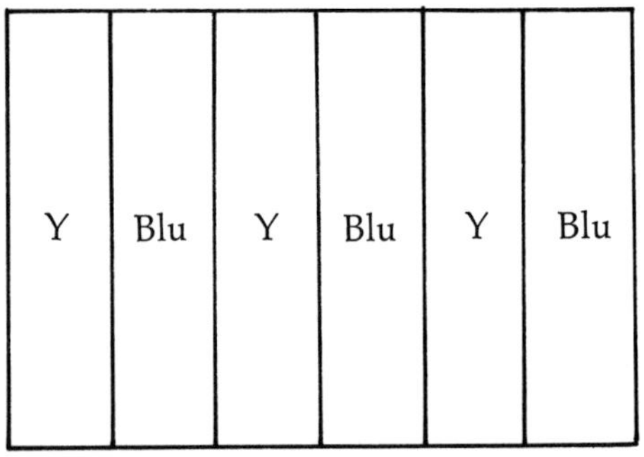

G

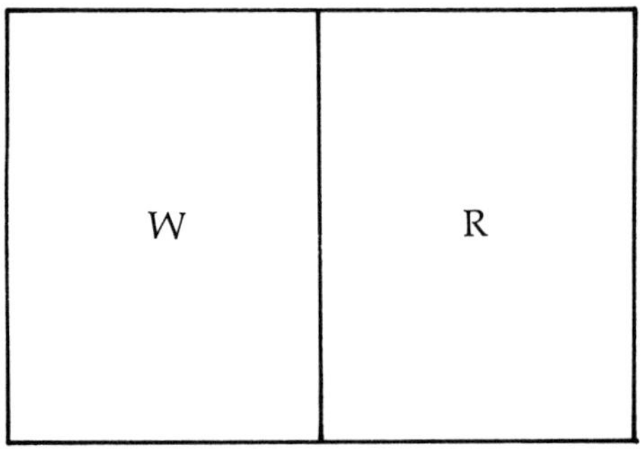

H

White—W Yellow—Y Black—Bk
Red—R Blue—Blu

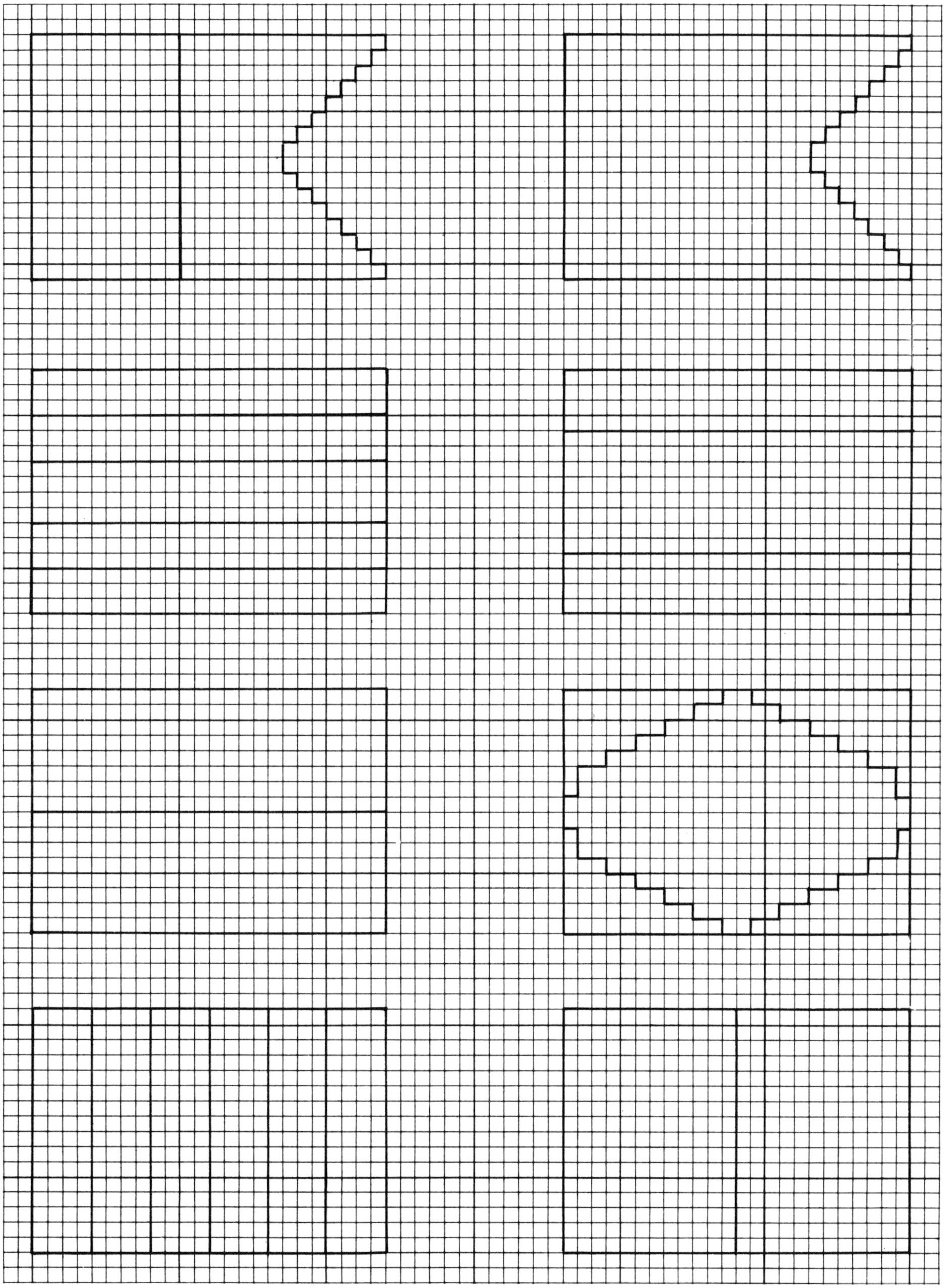

See Plate 2

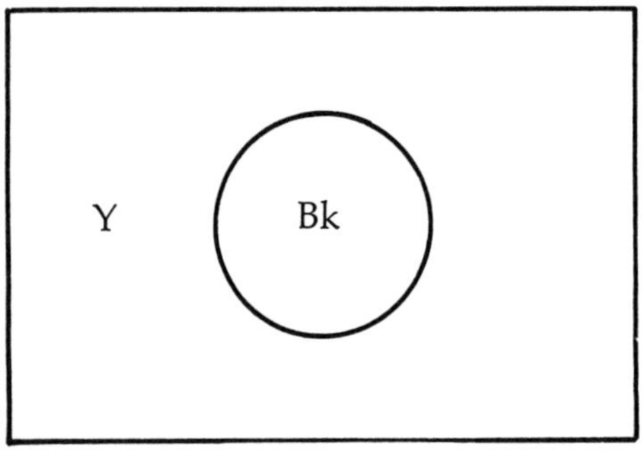
Y
Bk

I

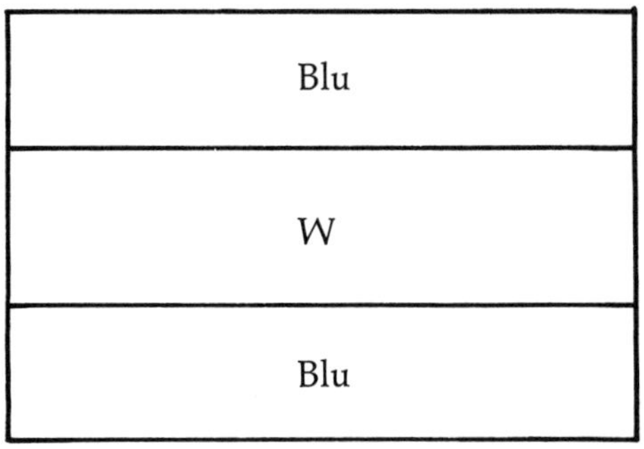
Blu
W
Blu

J

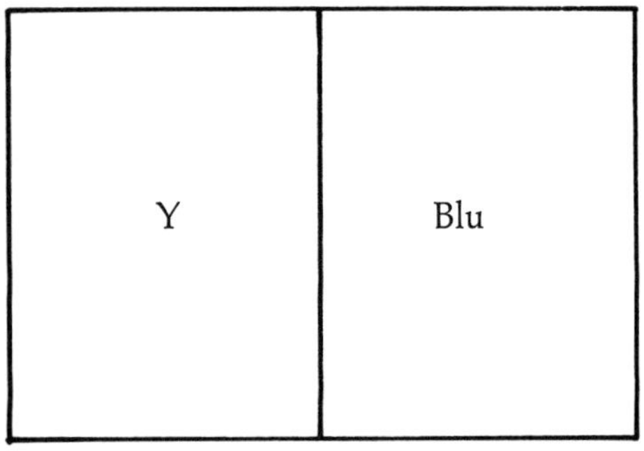
Y
Blu

K

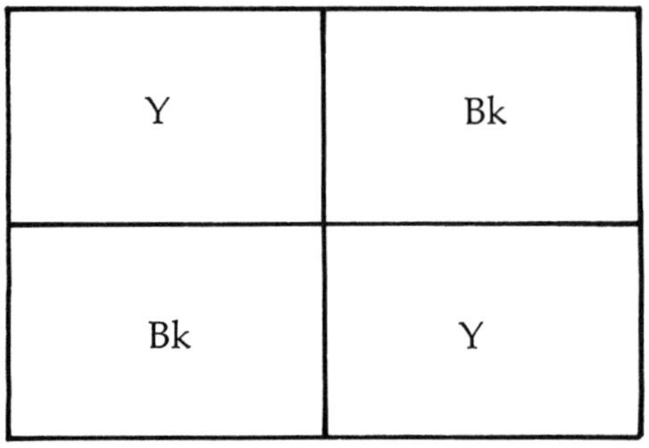
Y
Bk
Bk
Y

L

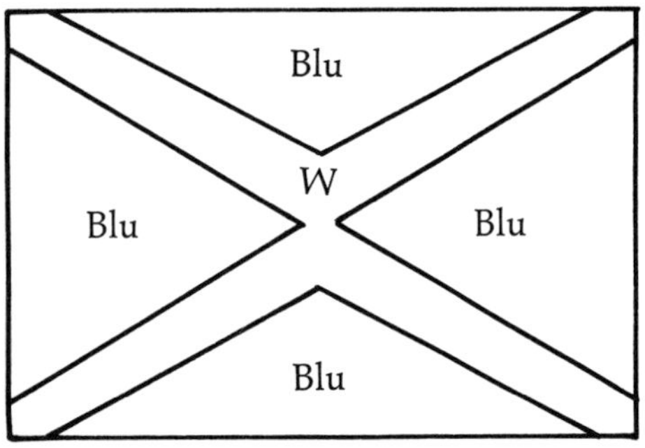
Blu
W
Blu
Blu
Blu

M

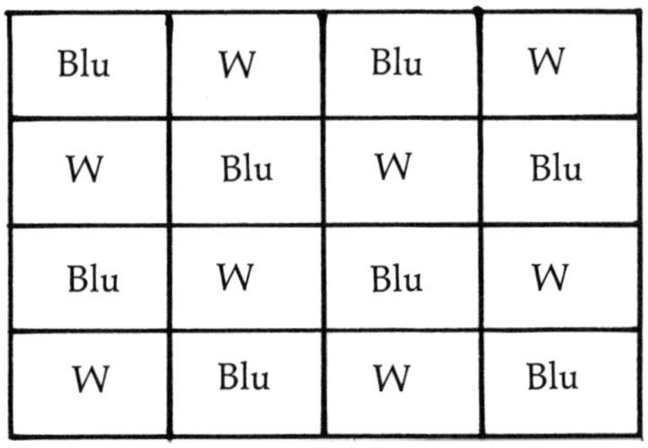
Blu
W
Blu
W
W
Blu
W
Blu
Blu
W
Blu
W
W
Blu
W
Blu

N

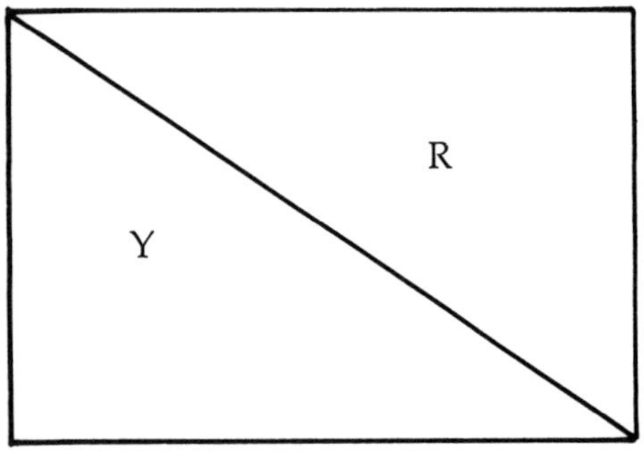
R
Y

O

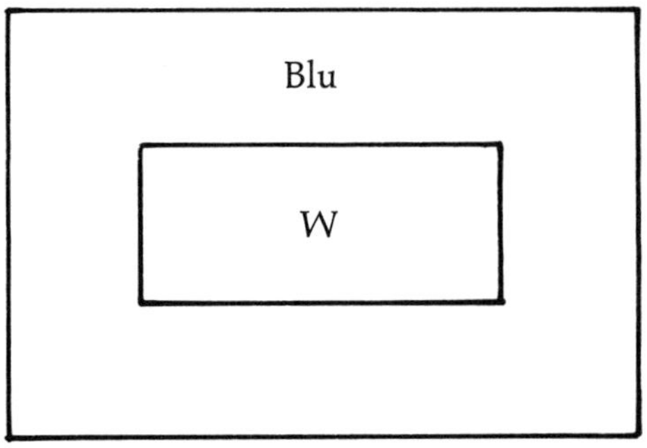
Blu
W

P

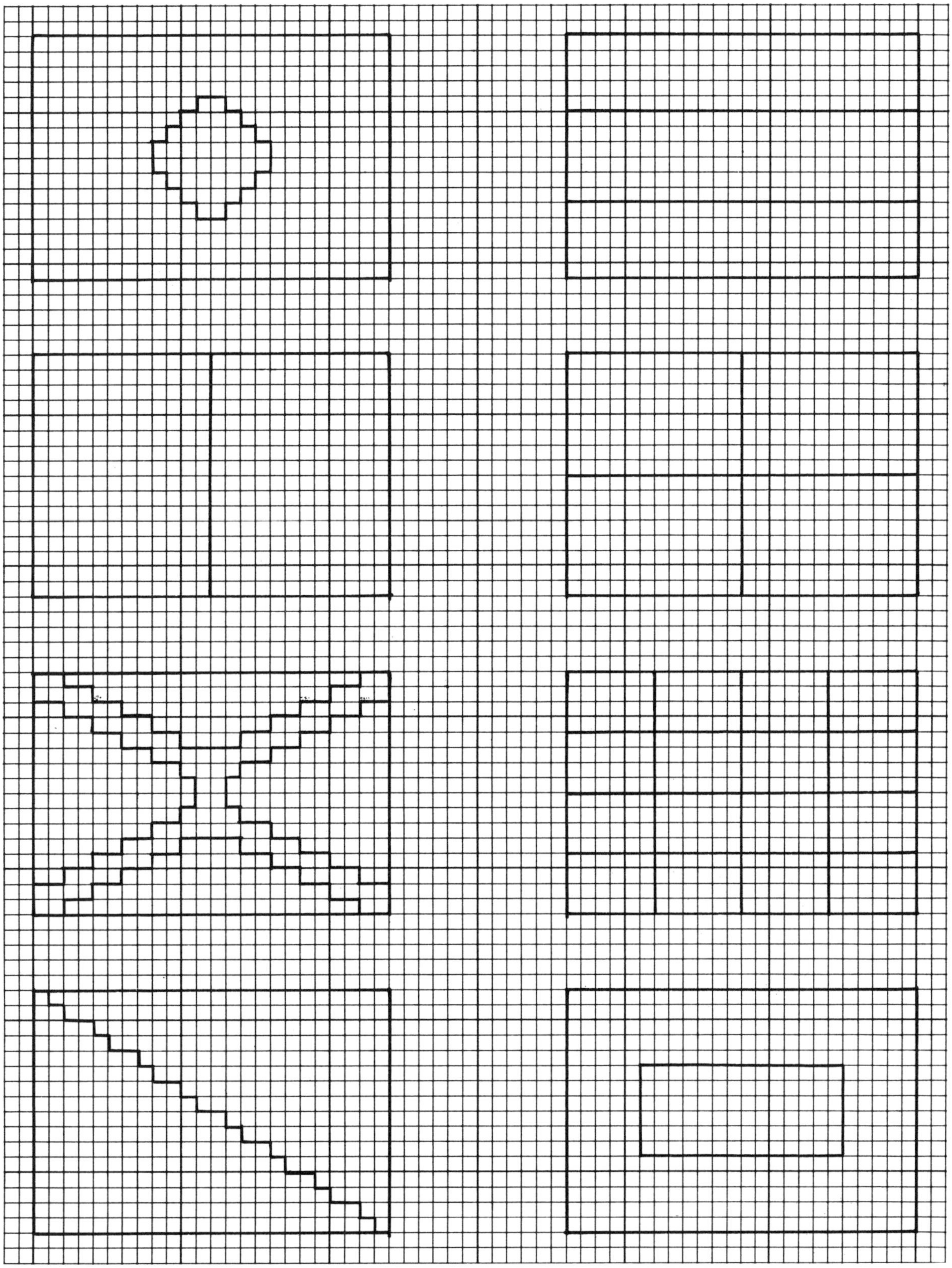

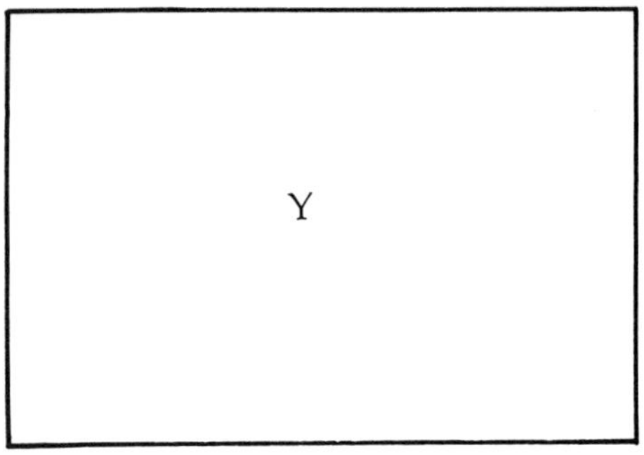
Y

Q

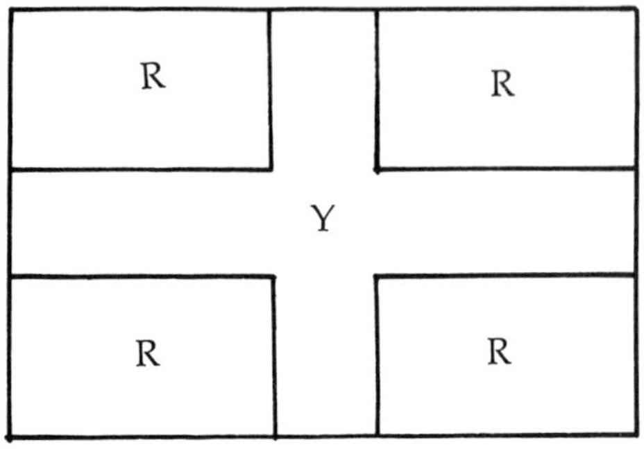
R
R
Y
R
R

R

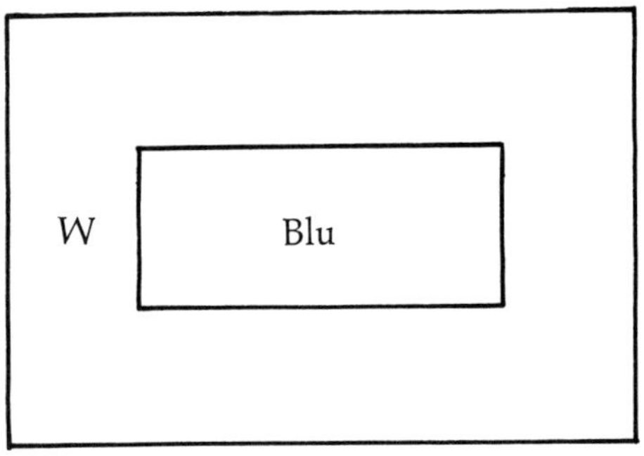
W
Blu

S

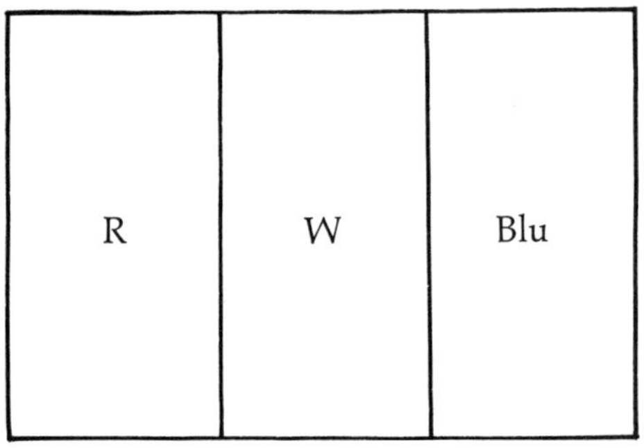
R
W
Blu

T

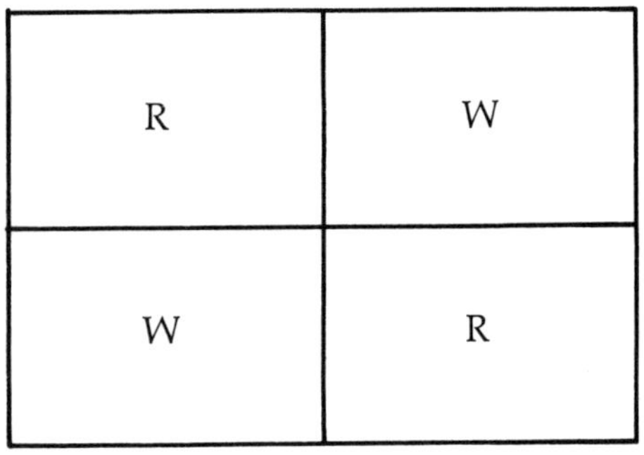
R
W
W
R

U

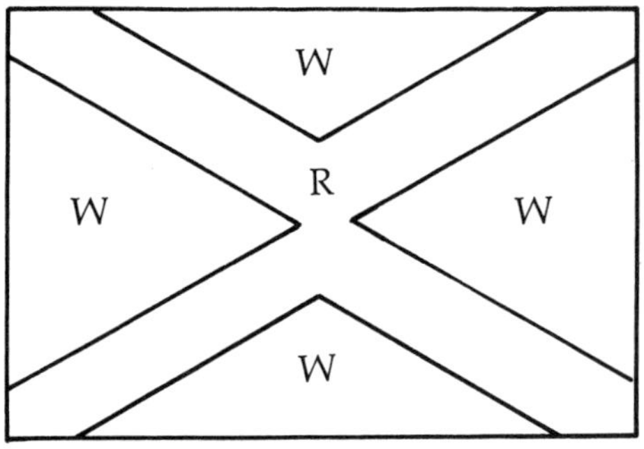
W
R
W
W
W

V

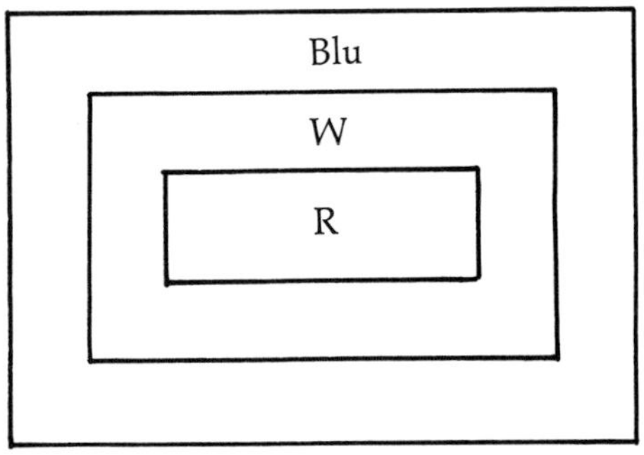
Blu
W
R

W

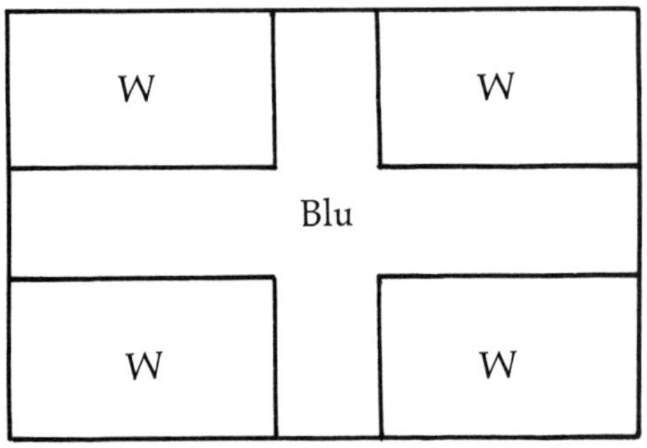
W
W
Blu
W
W

X

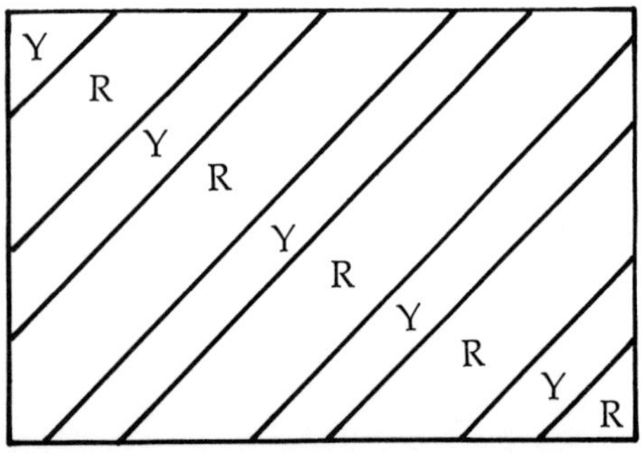
Y
R
Y
R
Y
R
Y
R
Y
R

Y

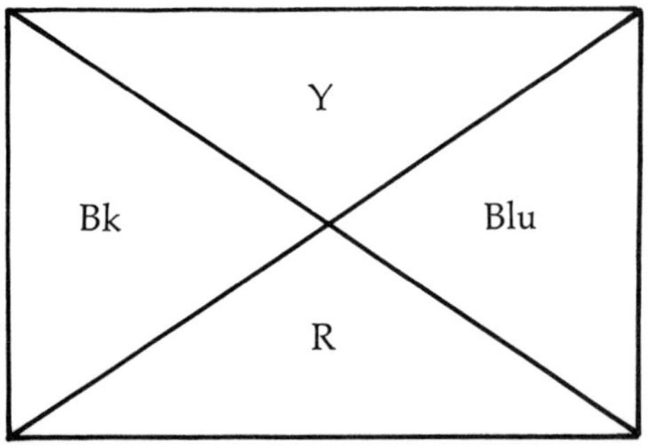
Y
Bk
Blu
R

Z

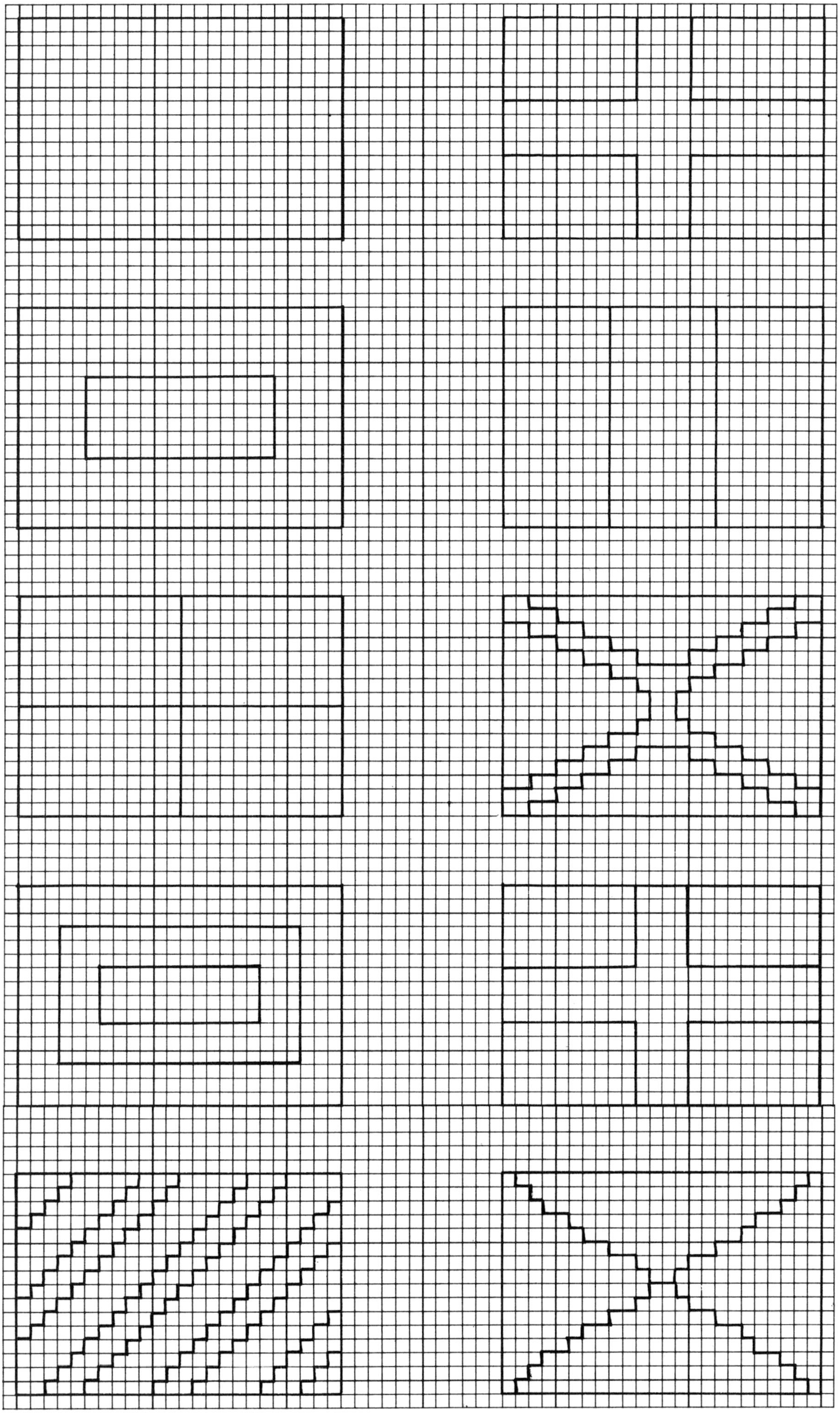

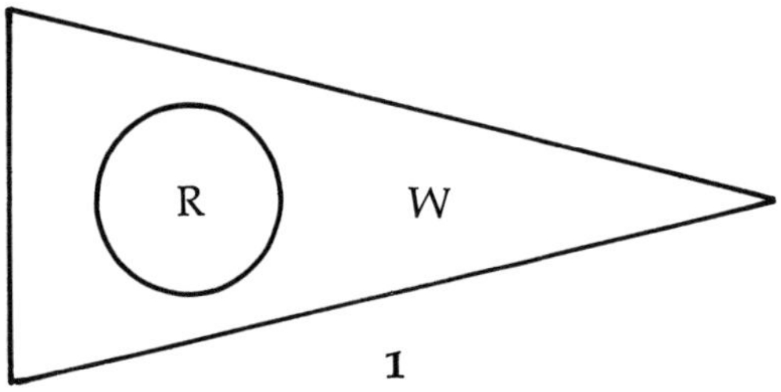

1

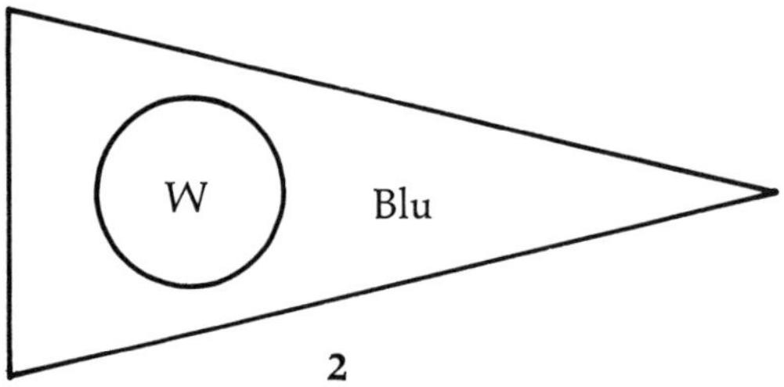

2

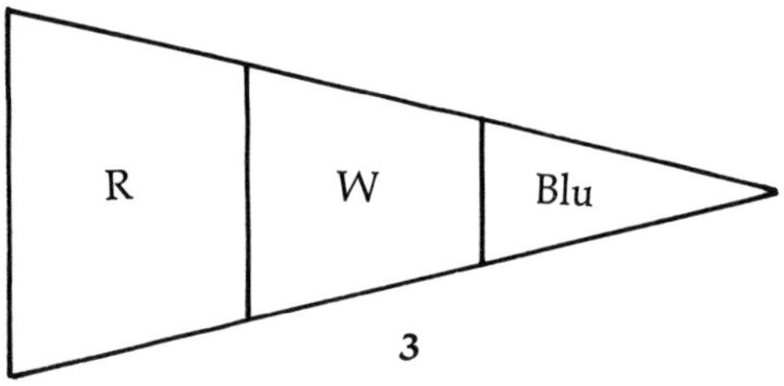

3

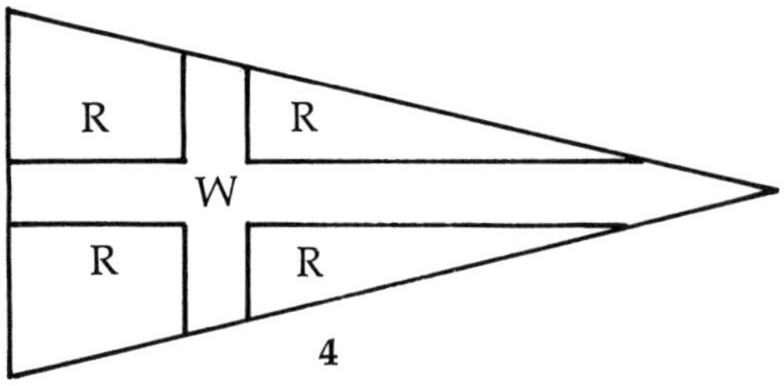

4

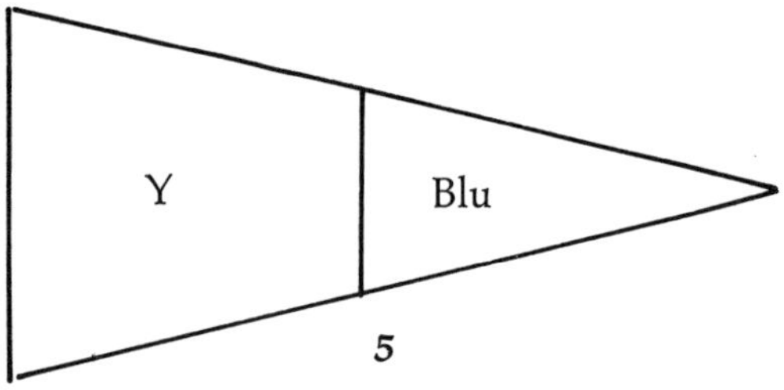

5

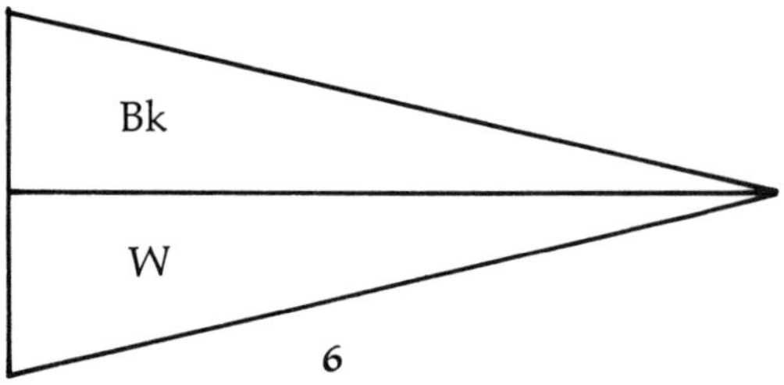

6

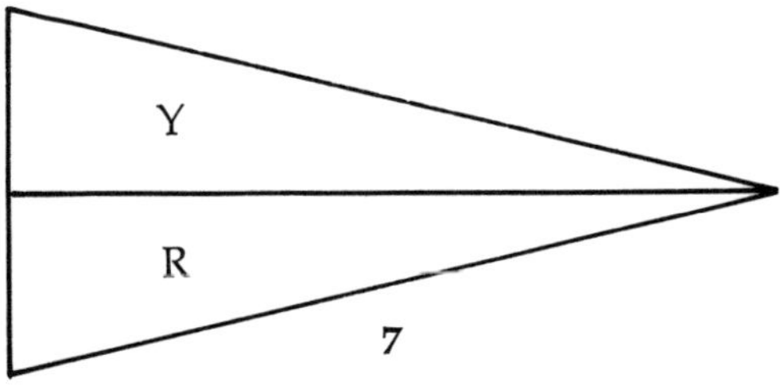

7

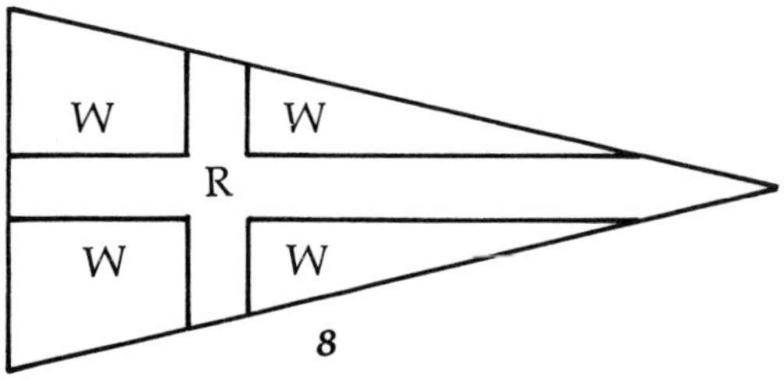

8

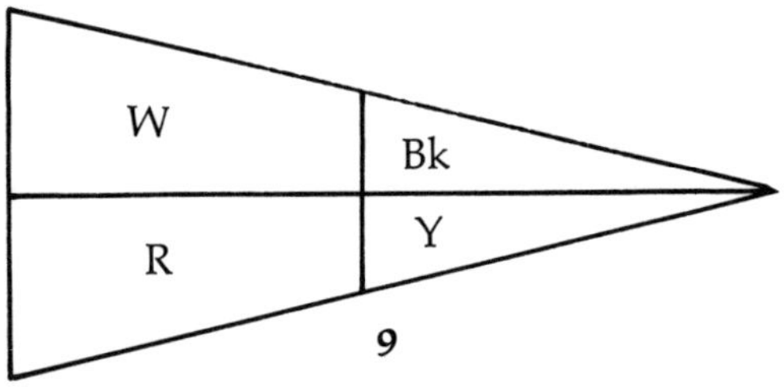

9

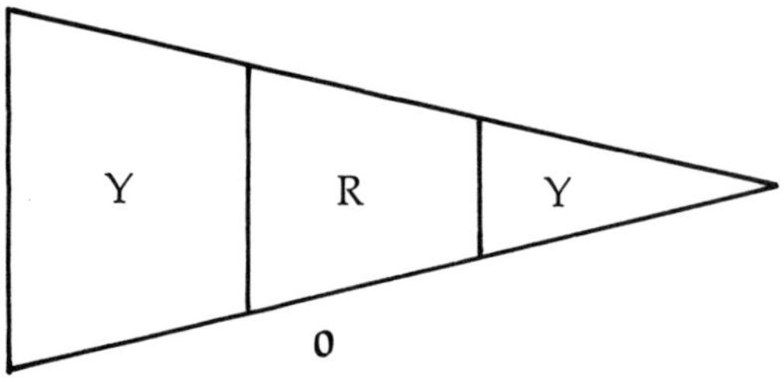

0

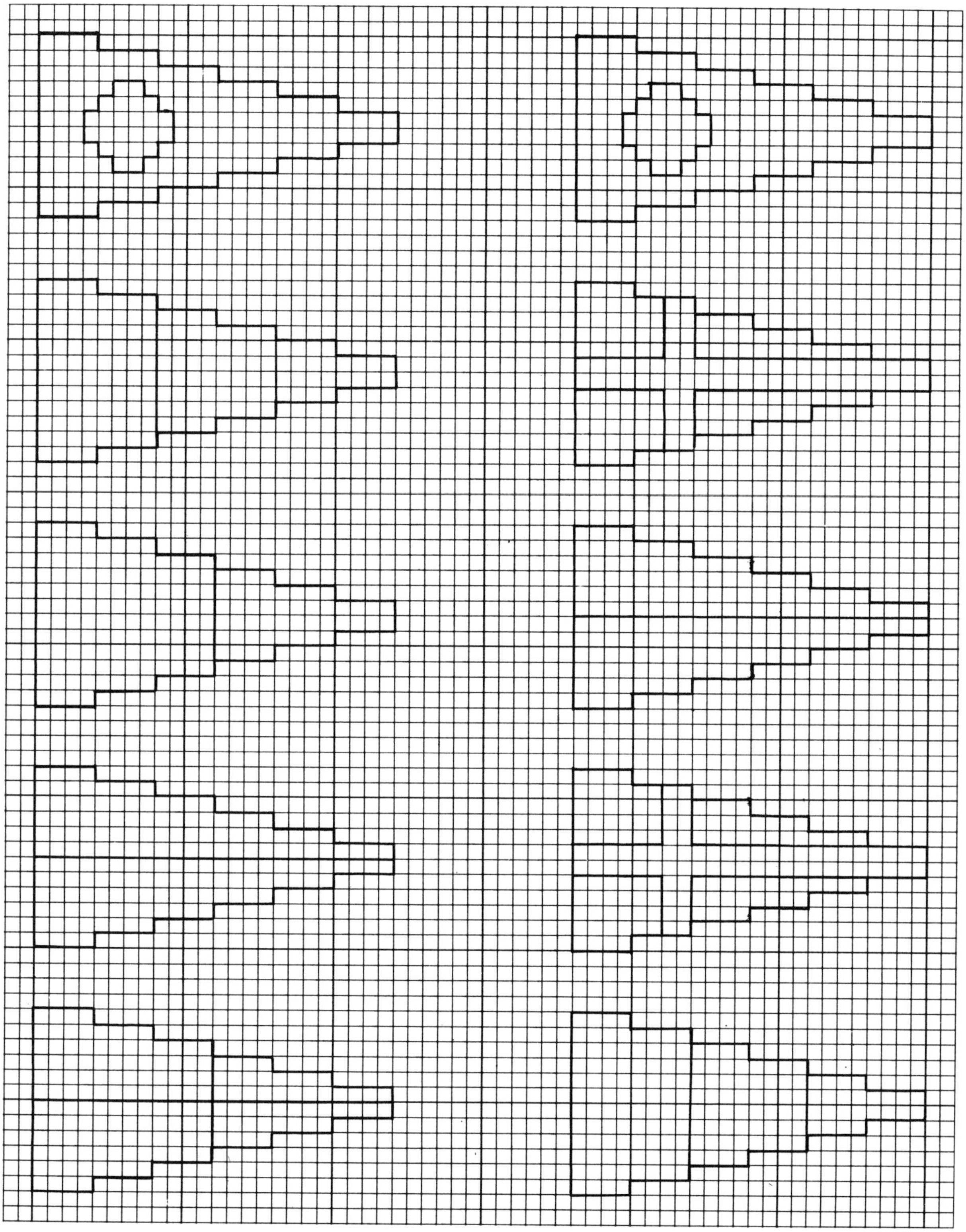

¼″ graph

½″ graph

¾″ graph